Christmas Origami

Other books by John Montroll:

Origami Sculptures

Prehistoric Origami *Dinosaurs and Other Creatures*

Origami Sea Life by John Montroll and Robert J. Lang

African Animals in Origami

North American Animals in Origami

Mythological Creatures and the Chinese Zodiac in Origami

Teach Yourself Origami

Bringing Origami to Life

Dollar Bill Animals in Origami

Bugs and Birds in Origami

A Plethora of Polyhedra in Origami

Dollar Bill Origami

A Constellation of Origami Polyhedra

Animal Origami for the Enthusiast

Origami for the Enthusiast

Easy Origami

Birds in Origami

Favorite Animals in Origami

Easy Christmas Origami

Christmas Origami

John Montroll

Dover Publications, Inc.
New York

To Cindy

Bibliographical Note

This work is first published in 2006 in separate editions by Antroll Publishing Company, Maryland, and Dover Publications, Inc., Mineola, New York.

International Standard Book Number: 0-486-45025-2

Manufactured in the United States of America
Dover Publications, Inc., 31 East 2nd Street, Mineola, N.Y. 11501

Introduction

"T was the night before Christmas and all through the house . . . ." Each year, friends and family around the world come together to celebrate the joyous holiday of Christmas and an exciting part of Christmas preparations is making decorations for the house and tree.

I am pleased to present 47 Christmas projects, most at the intermediate folding level. Models are grouped into four sections: the Nativity, Twelve Days of Christmas, Tree Ornaments and Gifts, and the North Pole. Each section contains exciting models that bring out the spirit of Christmas.

From the manger to the Three Wise Men, the Nativity scene reflects the meaning of Christmas. In the Twelve Days of Christmas section, folders will delight in making everything from the partridge to the twelve drummers drumming, with the five golden rings in the middle. In the Tree Ornaments and Gift section, which includes an angel and gift boxes, decorate your tree and house with a train set, stockings, and even the nutcracker. To round out the book, visit the North Pole where you will find trees, snowman, reindeer, and of course Santa Claus.

Each model is folded from a single sheet of uncut paper. The difficulty level, though somewhat arbitrary, is shown in the contents. It is recommended that a beginner start with simple, one star models. The illustrations conform to the internationally accepted Randlett-Yoshizawa conventions. The colored side of origami paper is represented by the shadings in the diagrams. Origami paper can be found in many hobby shops or purchased by mail from OrigamiUSA, 15 West 77th Street, New York, NY 10024-5192 or from Dover Publications, Inc., 31 East 2nd Street, Mineola, NY 11501. Large sheets are easier to use than small ones.

Many people helped with this project. In particular, I thank my editors, Jan Polish and Charley Montroll. I also thank the many folders who proof read the diagrams.

John Montroll

Contents

Symbols 10
Basic Folds 11

★ Simple
★★ Intermediate
★★★ Complex

Nativity *page 13*

Manger
★★
page 14

**Star of
Bethlehem**
★★
page 16

Palm Tree
★★
page 19

Mary
★★
page 22

**Joseph or
Shepherd with Cane**
★★
page 24

Wise Man
★★
page 25

Baby Jesus
★★
page 26

Cradle
★★
page 27

Dog
★★★
page 29

Dromedary
★★★
page 32

Sheep
★★★
page 35

Cow
★★★
page 38

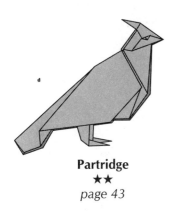

Partridge
★★
page 43

Turtle Dove
★★
page 45

French Hen
★★
page 47

Calling Bird
★
page 49

Golden Ring
★
page 51

Goose
★★
page 52

Swan
★★
page 54

Maid a-Milking
★★
page 55

Ladies Dancing
★★
page 58

Lord a-Leaping
★★
page 59

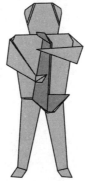

Pipers Piping
★★
page 62

Drummers Drumming
★★
page 64

More →

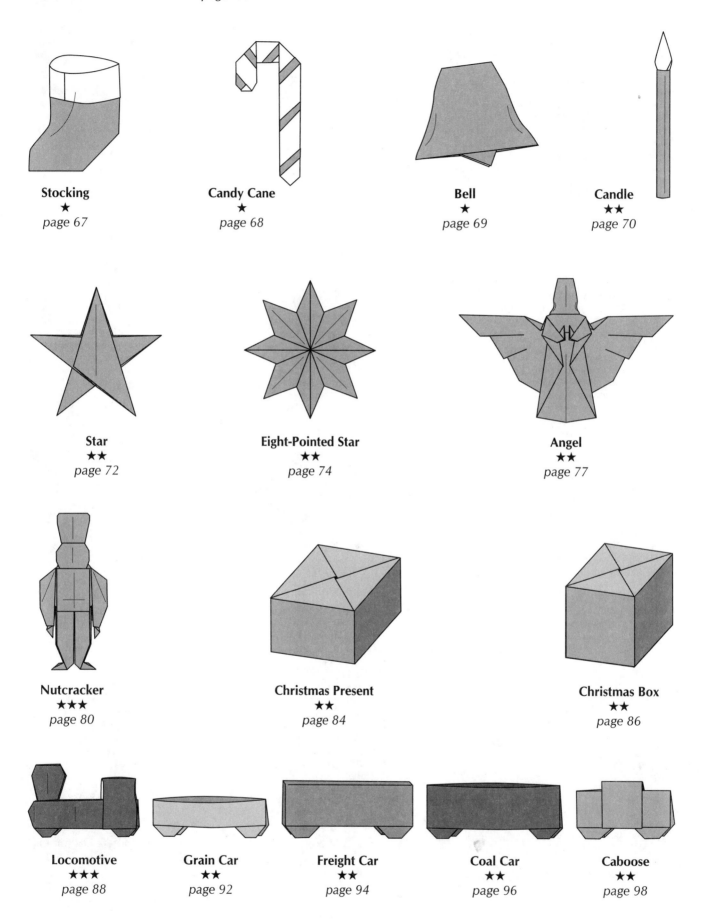

Stocking
★
page 67

Candy Cane
★
page 68

Bell
★
page 69

Candle
★★
page 70

Star
★★
page 72

Eight-Pointed Star
★★
page 74

Angel
★★
page 77

Nutcracker
★★★
page 80

Christmas Present
★★
page 84

Christmas Box
★★
page 86

Locomotive
★★★
page 88

Grain Car
★★
page 92

Freight Car
★★
page 94

Coal Car
★★
page 96

Caboose
★★
page 98

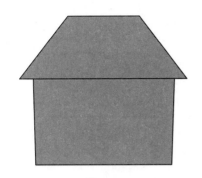

House
★
page 101

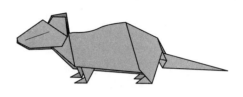

Mouse
★★
page 102

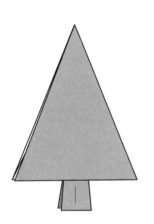

Christmas Tree
★★
page 106

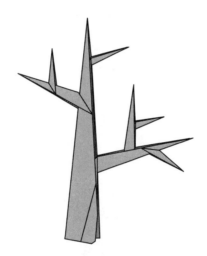

Winter Tree
★★
page 108

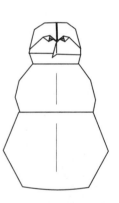

Snowman
★★
page 111

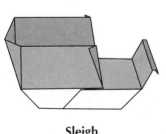

Sleigh
★★★
page 113

Reindeer
★★★
page 116

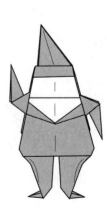

Santa Claus
★★★
page 118

Symbols

Lines

— — — — — — — — —   Valley fold, fold in front.

—·—·—·—·—·—·—   Mountain fold, fold behind.

————————   Crease line.

·····················   X-ray or guide line.

Arrows

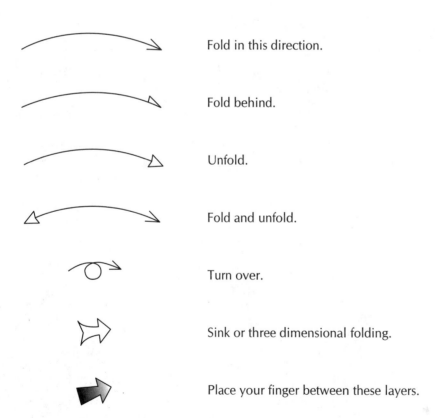

Fold in this direction.

Fold behind.

Unfold.

Fold and unfold.

Turn over.

Sink or three dimensional folding.

Place your finger between these layers.

Basic Folds

Rabbit Ear.

To fold a rabbit ear, one corner is folded in half and laid down to a side.

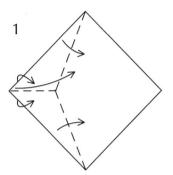

1

Fold a rabbit ear.

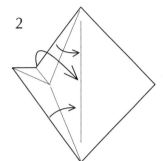

2

A three-dimensional
intermediate step.

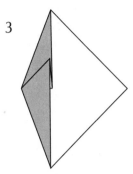

3

Squash Fold.

In a squash fold, some paper is opened and then made flat. The shaded arrow shows where to place your finger.

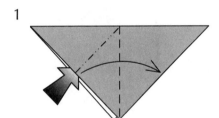

1

Squash-fold.

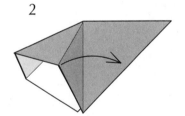

2

A three-dimensional
intermediate step.

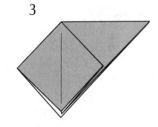

3

Petal Fold.

In a petal fold, one point is folded up while two opposite sides meet each other.

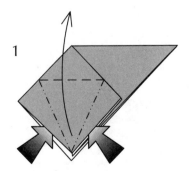

1

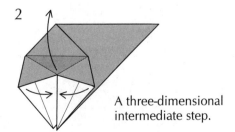

2

A three-dimensional
intermediate step.

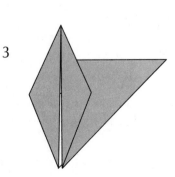

3

Inside Reverse Fold.

In an inside reverse fold, some paper is folded between layers. Here are two examples.

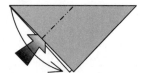

1

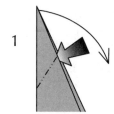

1

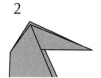

2

Reverse-fold.

Reverse-fold.

2

Outside Reverse Fold.

Much of the paper must be unfolded to make an outside reverse fold.

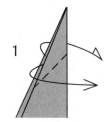

1

2

Outside-reverse-fold.

Crimp Fold.

A crimp fold is a combination of two reverse folds.

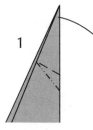

1

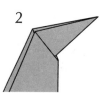

2

Crimp-fold.

Sink Fold.

In a sink fold, some of the paper without edges is folded inside. To do this fold, much of the model must be unfolded.

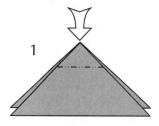

1

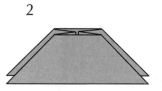

2

Sink.

Spread Squash Fold.

A cross between a squash fold and sink fold, some paper in the center is spread apart and then made flat.

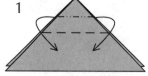

1

2

Spread-squash-fold.

Nativity

Manger

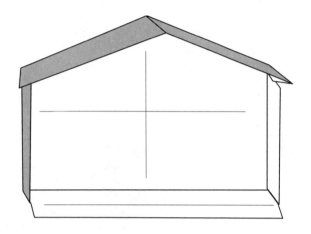

Away in a manger,
no crib for His bed,
The little Lord Jesus
laid down His sweet head;
The stars in the heavens
looked down where He lay,
The little Lord Jesus
asleep on the hay.

1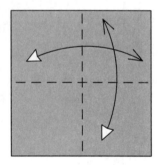

Fold and unfold.

2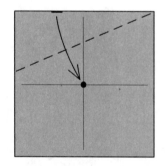

Bring the edge to the center.

3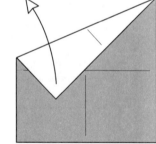

Unfold.

4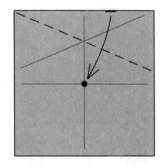

Repeat steps 2–3 on the right.

5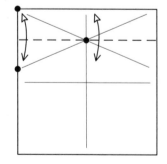

Fold and unfold.

6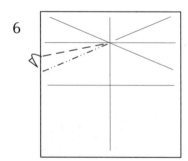

7

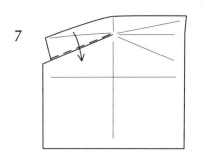

The model is three-dimensional.
Crease on the left.

8

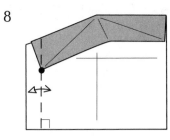

Fold and unfold.

9

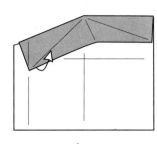

Lift up.

10

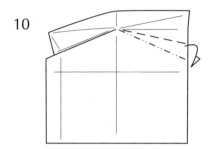

Repeat steps 6–9 on the right.

11

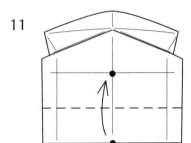

12

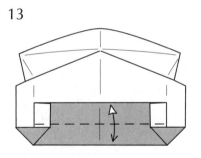

Squash folds.

13

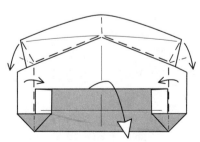

Fold and unfold.

14

Open and shape.

15

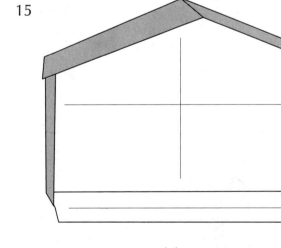

Manger

Star of Bethlehem

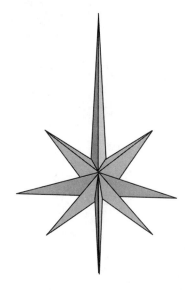

O star of wonder, star of night,
Star with royal beauty bright,
Westward leading, still proceeding,
Guide us to thy perfect Light.

1

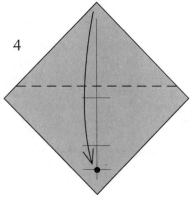

Fold and unfold.

2

Fold and unfold
in the center.

3

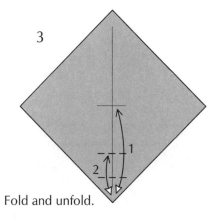

Fold and unfold.

4

Fold and unfold.

5

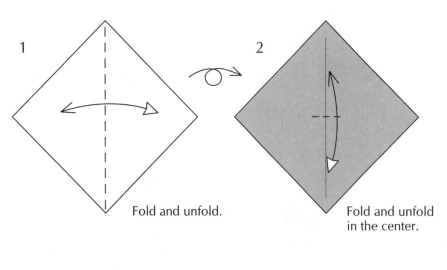

6

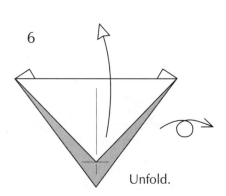

Unfold.

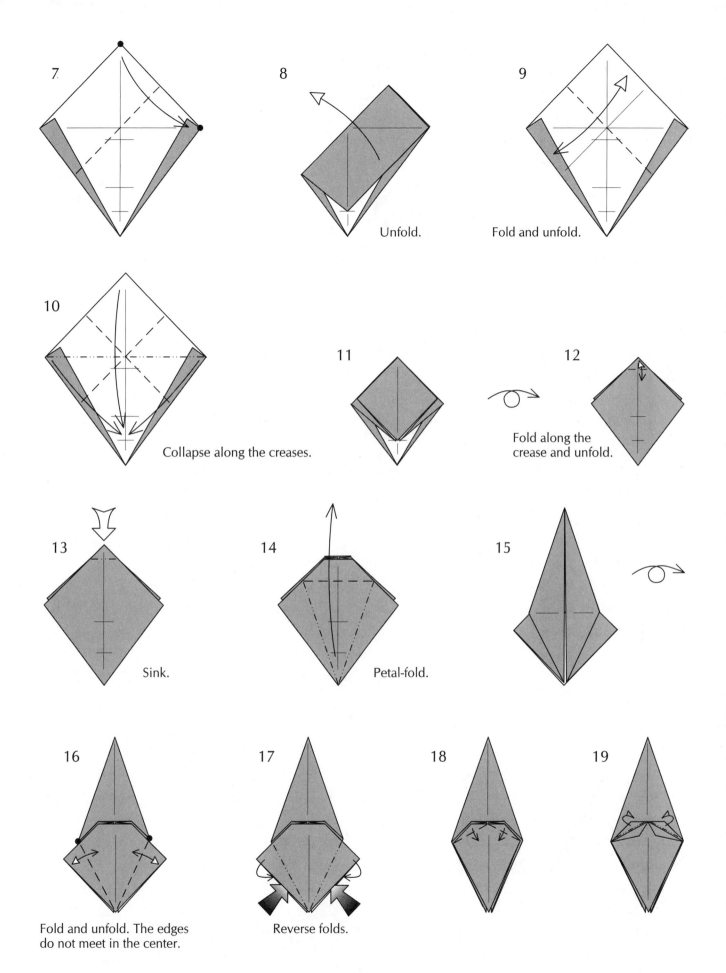

7

8

Unfold.

9

Fold and unfold.

10

Collapse along the creases.

11

12

Fold along the
crease and unfold.

13

Sink.

14

Petal-fold.

15

16

Fold and unfold. The edges
do not meet in the center.

17

Reverse folds.

18

19

20

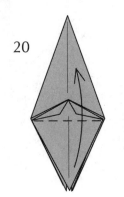

21

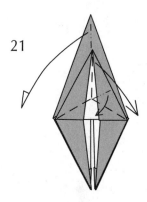

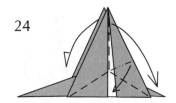

Rabbit-ear in front and behind.

22

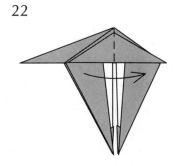

Repeat behind.

23

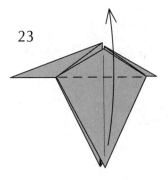

Repeat behind.

24

Rabbit-ear in front and behind.

25

Spread the eight points and rotate. The star will become three-dimensional.

26

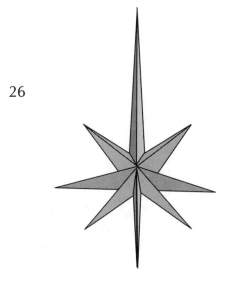

Star of Bethlehem

Palm Tree

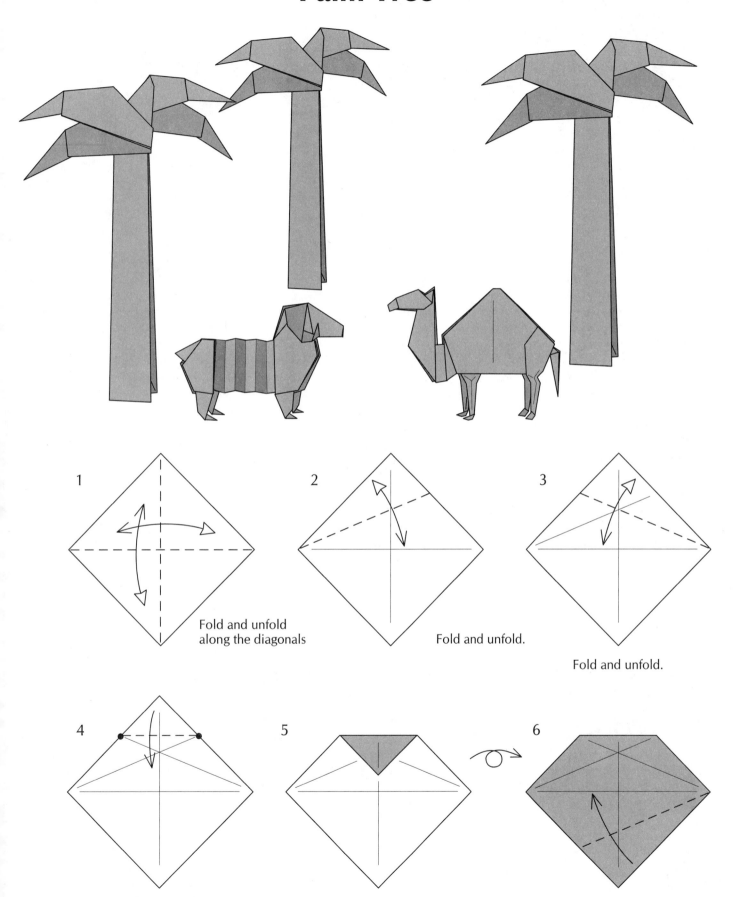

1

Fold and unfold
along the diagonals

2

Fold and unfold.

3

Fold and unfold.

4

5

6

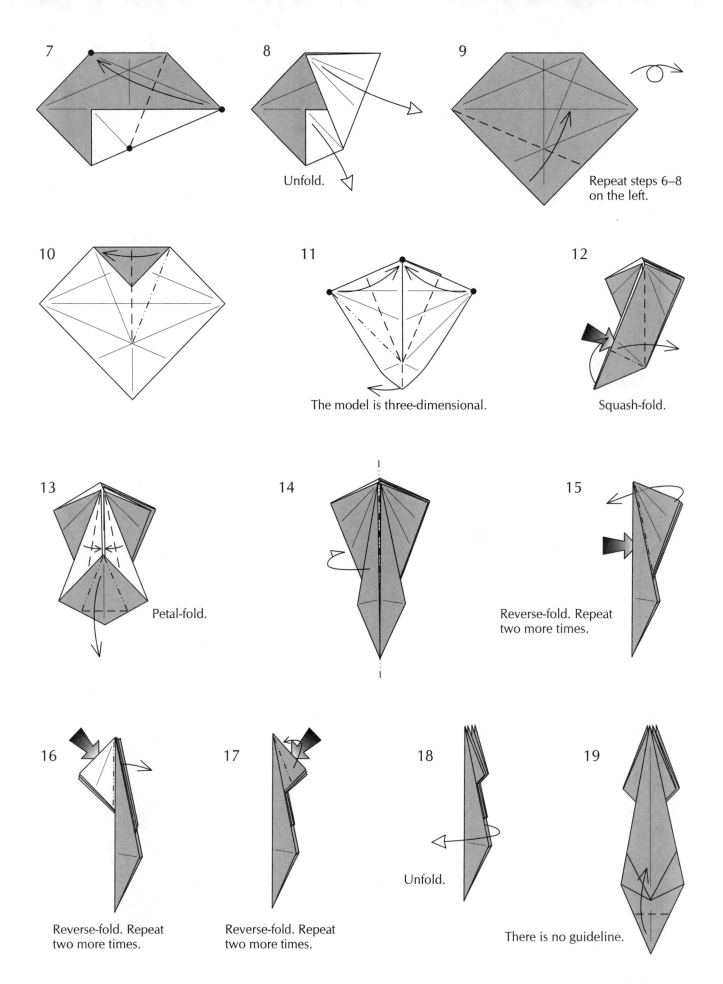

7

8

Unfold.

9

Repeat steps 6–8 on the left.

10

11

The model is three-dimensional.

12

Squash-fold.

13

Petal-fold.

14

15

Reverse-fold. Repeat two more times.

16

Reverse-fold. Repeat two more times.

17

Reverse-fold. Repeat two more times.

18

Unfold.

19

There is no guideline.

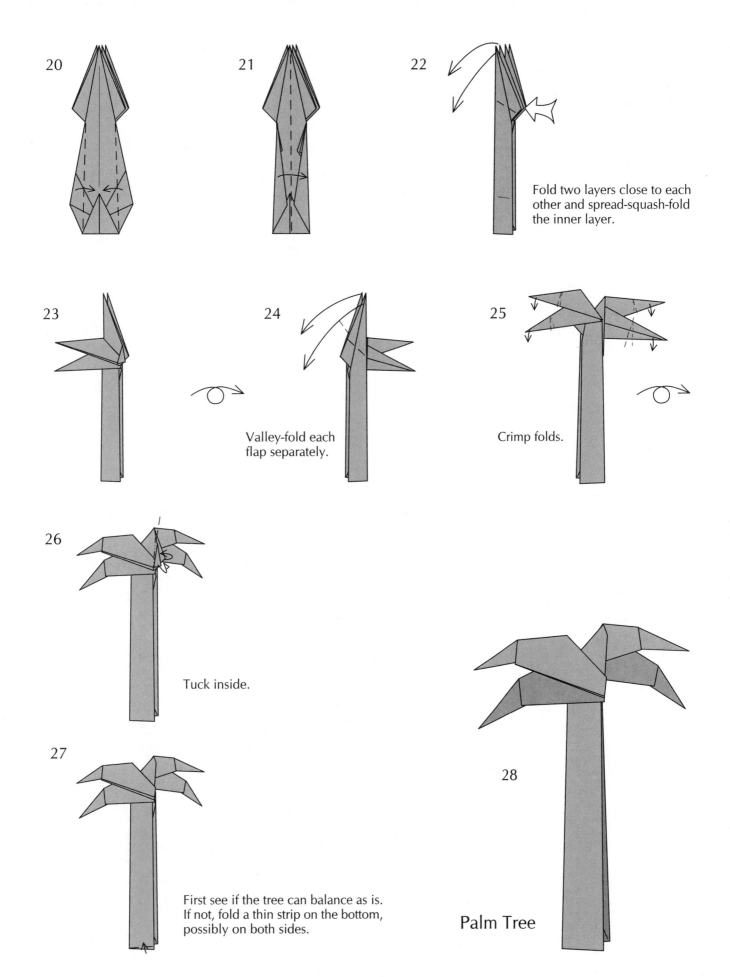

20

21

22 Fold two layers close to each other and spread-squash-fold the inner layer.

23

24 Valley-fold each flap separately.

25 Crimp folds.

26 Tuck inside.

27 First see if the tree can balance as is. If not, fold a thin strip on the bottom, possibly on both sides.

28 Palm Tree

Mary

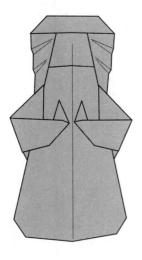

Silent night, holy night,
All is calm, all is bright
Round yon virgin mother and child.
Holy infant so tender and mild,
Sleep in heavenly peace.
Sleep in heavenly peace.

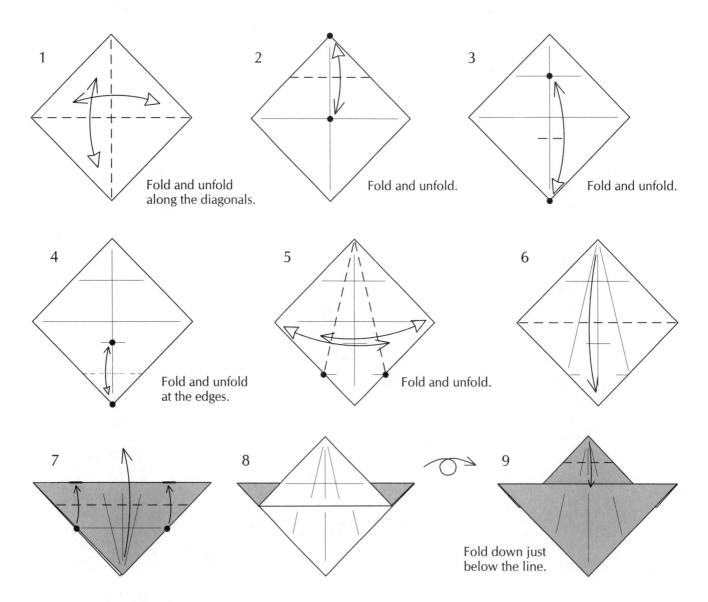

1 Fold and unfold along the diagonals.

2 Fold and unfold.

3 Fold and unfold.

4 Fold and unfold at the edges.

5 Fold and unfold.

6

7

8

9 Fold down just below the line.

10

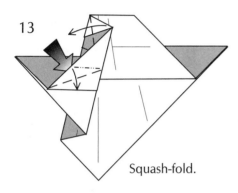

11

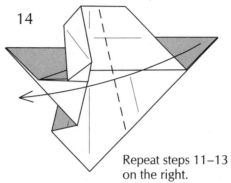

12

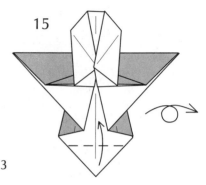

Fold. The crease exists between the dots, and should be continued to the edge of the paper.

13

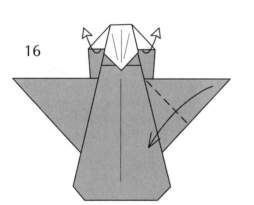

Squash-fold.

14

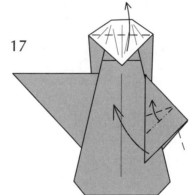

Repeat steps 11–13 on the right.

15

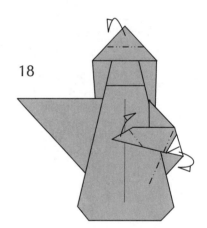

16

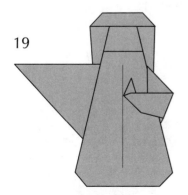

Pull out at the head.

17

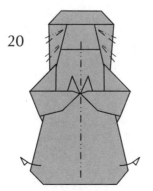

18

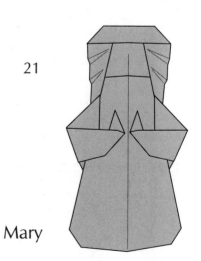

19

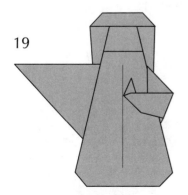

Repeat steps 16–18 for the arm on the left.

20

Bend slightly in half for the model to stand.

21

Mary

Joseph and Shepherd with Cane

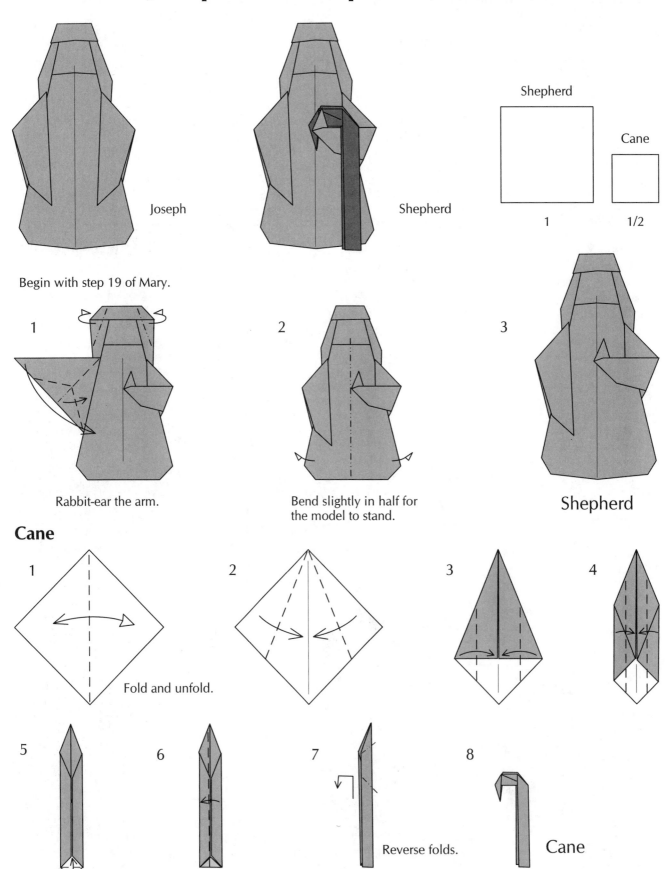

Joseph

Shepherd

Shepherd

Cane

1

1/2

Begin with step 19 of Mary.

1 Rabbit-ear the arm.

2 Bend slightly in half for the model to stand.

3 Shepherd

Cane

1 Fold and unfold.

2

3

4

5

6

7 Reverse folds.

8 Cane

Wise Man

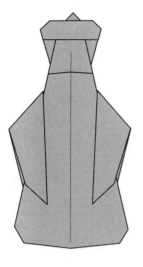

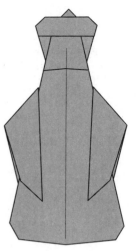

We three kings of Orient are
Bearing gifts we traverse afar.
Field and fountain, moor and mountain,
Following yonder star.

Begin with step 16 of Mary.

1

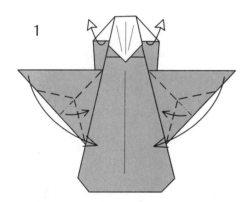

Pull out at the head and
rabbit-ear the arms.

2

3

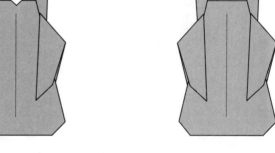

4

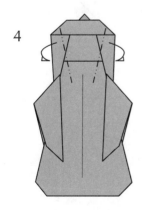

5

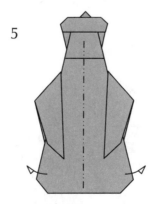

Bend slightly in half for
the model to stand.

6

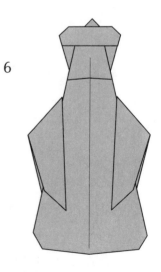

Wise Man

Baby Jesus

Come they told me, pa rum pum pum pum
A new born King to see, pa rum pum pum pum
Our finest gifts we bring, pa rum pum pum pum
To lay before the King, pa rum pum pum pum,
rum pum pum pum, rum pum pum pum,

So to honor Him, pa rum pum pum pum,
When we come.

Little Baby, pa rum pum pum pum
I am a poor boy too, pa rum pum pum pum
I have no gift to bring, pa rum pum pum pum
That's fit to give the King, pa rum pum pum pum,
rum pum pum pum, rum pum pum pum,

Shall I play for you, pa rum pum pum pum,
On my drum?

Mary nodded, pa rum pum pum pum
The ox and lamb kept time, pa rum pum pum pum
I played my drum for Him, pa rum pum pum pum
I played my best for Him, pa rum pum pum pum,
rum pum pum pum, rum pum pum pum,

Then He smiled at me, pa rum pum pum pum
Me and my drum.

10

Baby Jesus

Begin with step 9 of Mary.

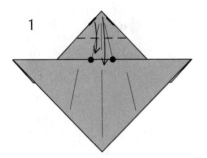

1

Fold down so the bold
edge is just above the dot.

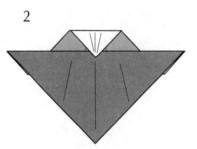

2

Bring the dark paper to the front.

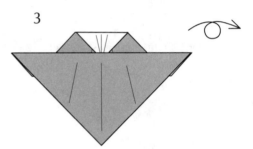

3

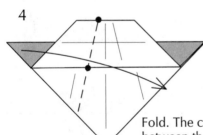

4

Fold. The crease exists
between the dots, and
should be continued to
the edge of the paper.

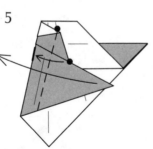

5

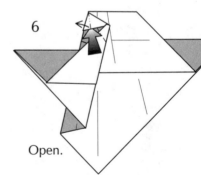

6

Open.

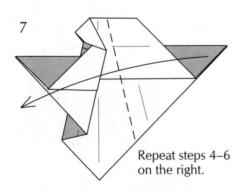

7

Repeat steps 4–6
on the right.

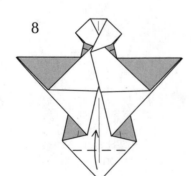

8

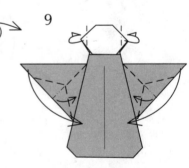

9

Rabbit-ear the arms.

Cradle

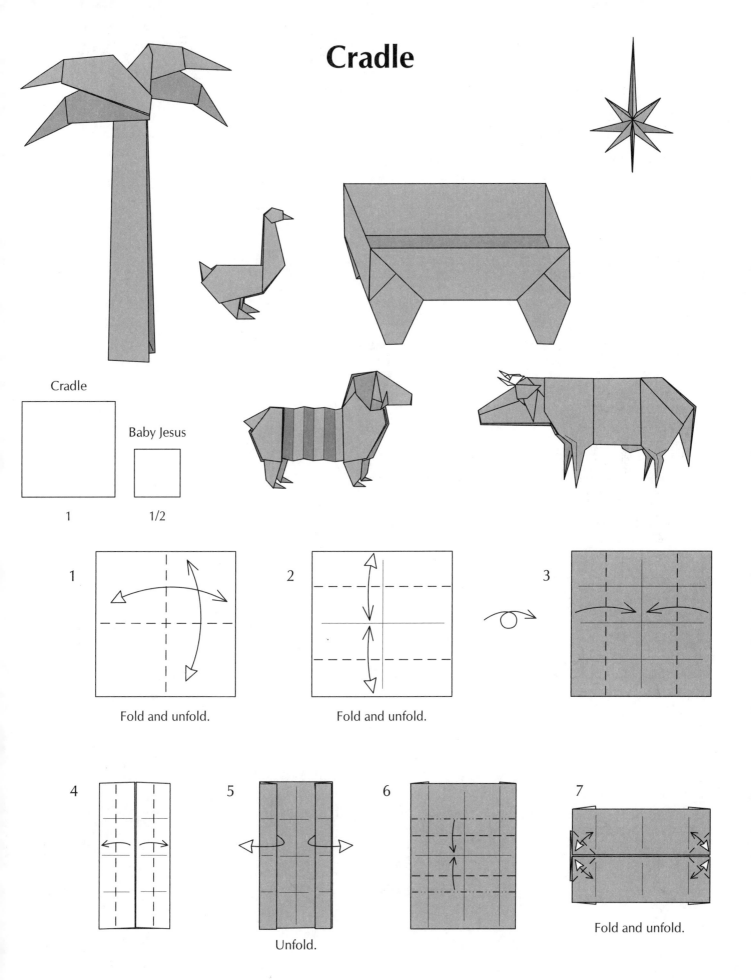

Cradle

1

Baby Jesus

1/2

1

Fold and unfold.

2

Fold and unfold.

3

4

5

Unfold.

6

7

Fold and unfold.

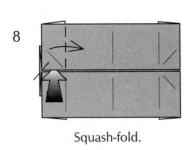

8

Squash-fold.

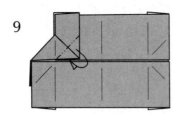

9

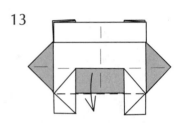

10

Repeat steps 7–9
three more times.

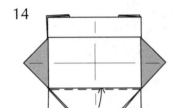

11

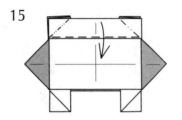

12

Petal-fold.

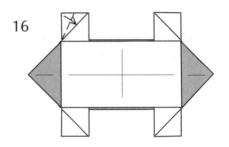

13

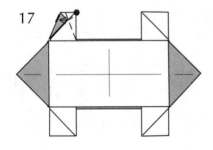

14

Tuck inside.

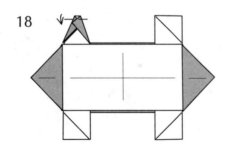

15

Repeat steps 12–14 at the top.

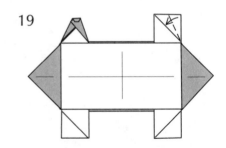

16

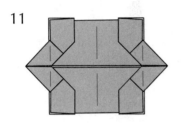

17

18

19

Repeat steps 16–18
three more times.

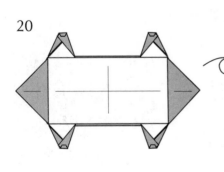

20

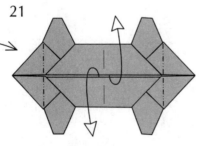

21

Open.

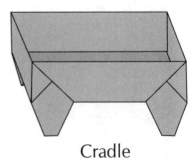

22

Cradle

Dog

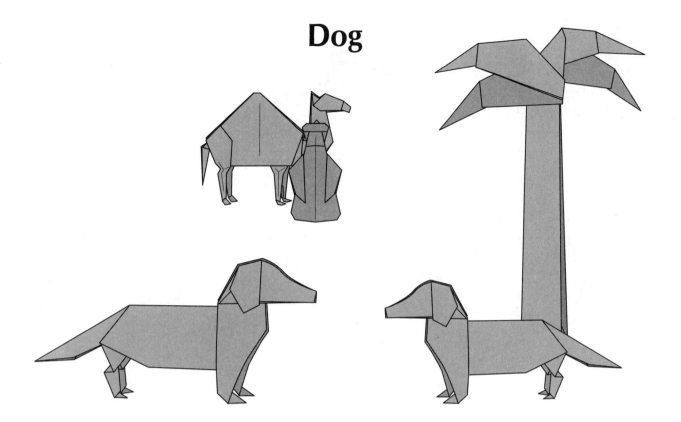

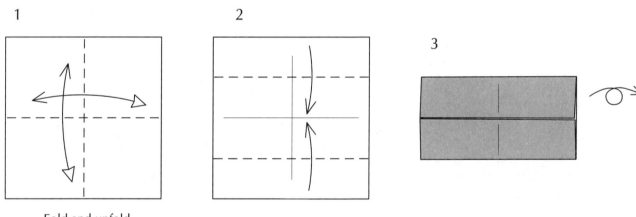

1

Fold and unfold.

2

3

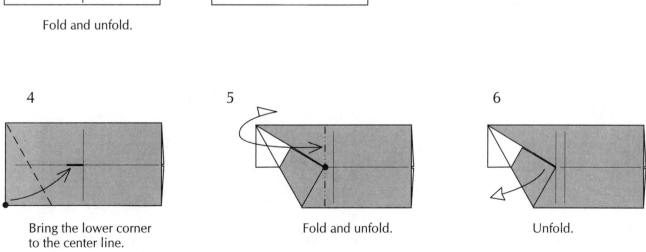

4

Bring the lower corner to the center line.

5

Fold and unfold.

6

Unfold.

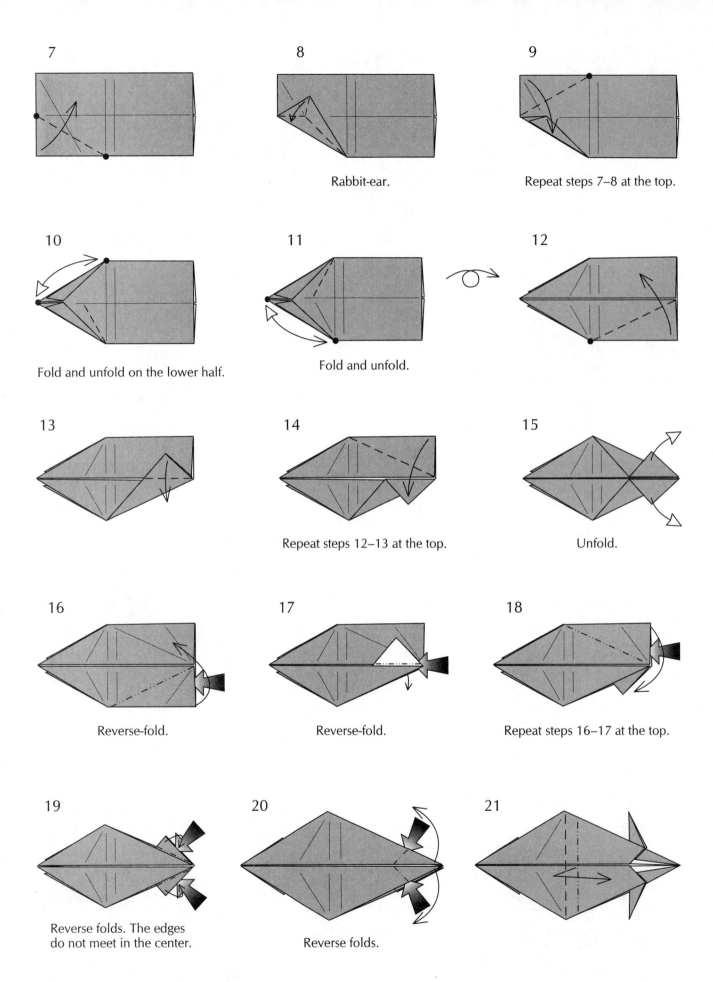

7

8

Rabbit-ear.

9

Repeat steps 7–8 at the top.

10

Fold and unfold on the lower half.

11

Fold and unfold.

12

13

14

Repeat steps 12–13 at the top.

15

Unfold.

16

Reverse-fold.

17

Reverse-fold.

18

Repeat steps 16–17 at the top.

19

Reverse folds. The edges
do not meet in the center.

20

Reverse folds.

21

22

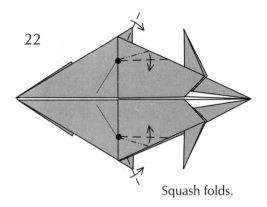

Squash folds.

23

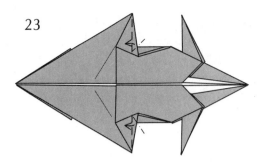

Squash folds.

24

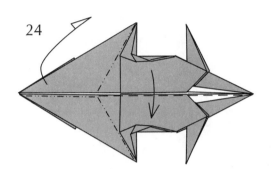

25

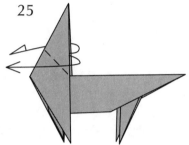

Outside-reverse-fold the head.

26

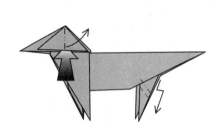

Open at the ear and crimp-fold the leg. Repeat behind.

27

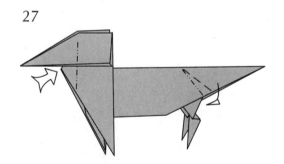

Sink the neck and crimp-fold the tail.

28

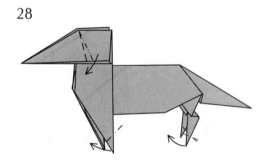

Form the ears, reverse-fold the front legs, and crimp-fold the hind legs. Repeat behind.

29

Reverse-fold the head and shape the ears. Shape the front legs and head. Repeat behind.

30

Dog

Dromedary

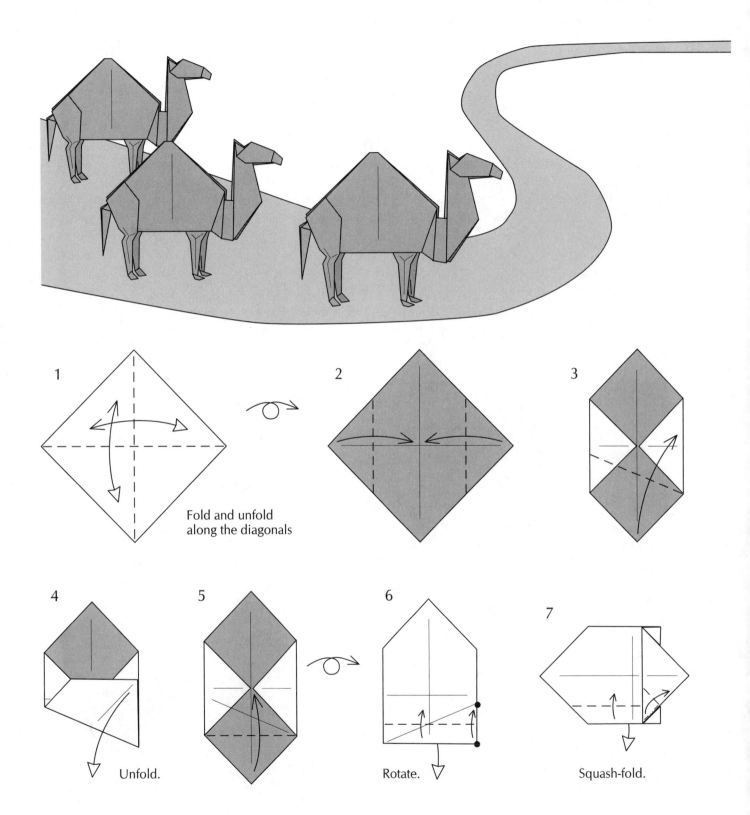

1 Fold and unfold along the diagonals

2

3

4 Unfold.

5

6 Rotate.

7 Squash-fold.

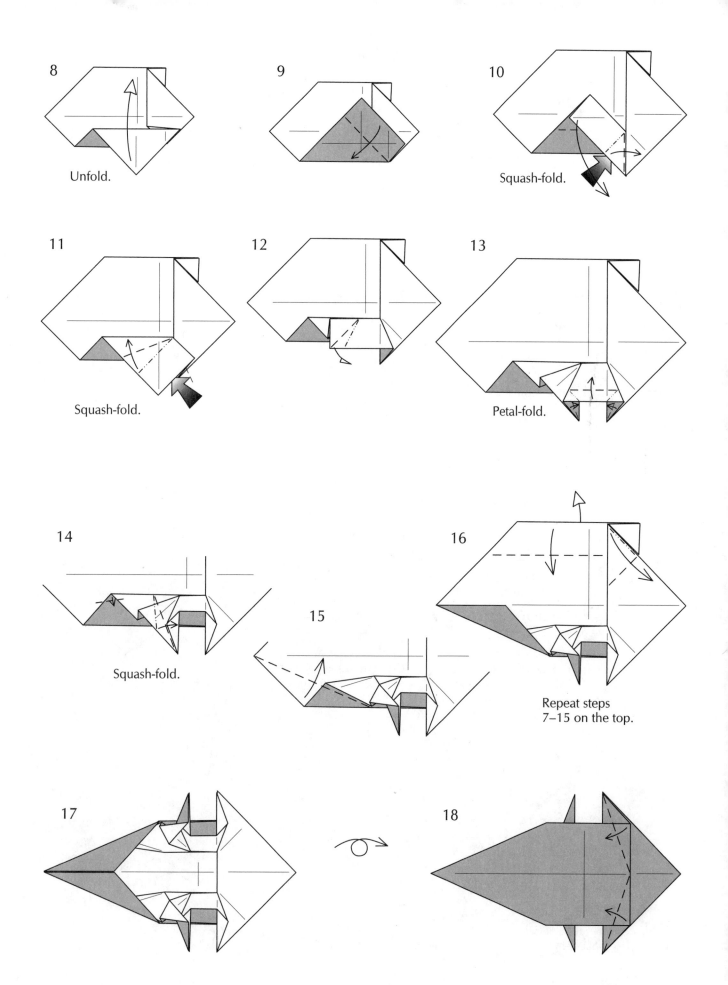

8

Unfold.

9

10

Squash-fold.

11

Squash-fold.

12

13

Petal-fold.

14

Squash-fold.

15

16

Repeat steps
7–15 on the top.

17

18

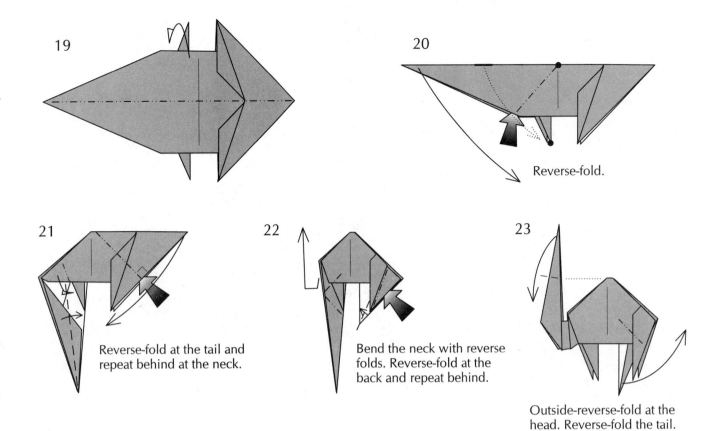

19

20

Reverse-fold.

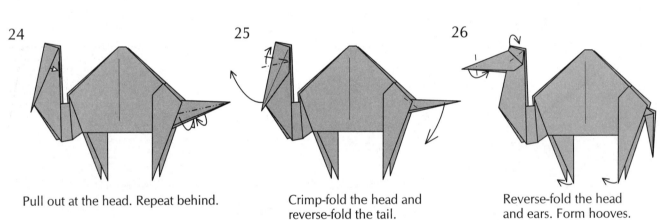

21

Reverse-fold at the tail and repeat behind at the neck.

22

Bend the neck with reverse folds. Reverse-fold at the back and repeat behind.

23

Outside-reverse-fold at the head. Reverse-fold the tail.

24

Pull out at the head. Repeat behind.

25

Crimp-fold the head and reverse-fold the tail.

26

Reverse-fold the head and ears. Form hooves.

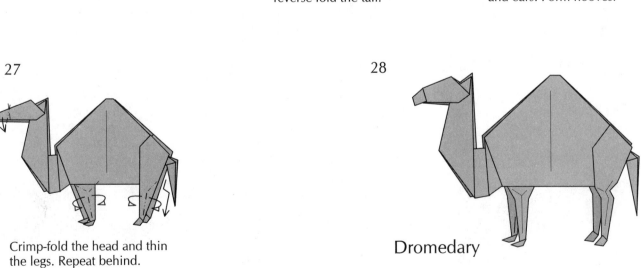

27

Crimp-fold the head and thin the legs. Repeat behind.

28

Dromedary

Sheep

The first Noel the angel did say
Was to certain poor shepherds in fields as they lay;
In fields as they lay, keeping their sheep,
On a cold winter's night that was so deep.
Noel, Noel, Noel, Noel,
Born is the King of Israel.

1

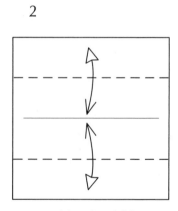

Fold and unfold.

2

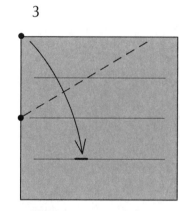

Fold and unfold.

3

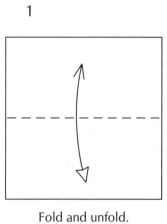

Fold the corner to the crease.

4

Unfold.

5

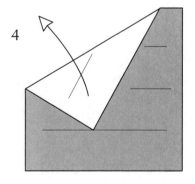

Fold and unfold.

6

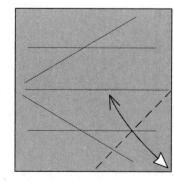

Fold and unfold.

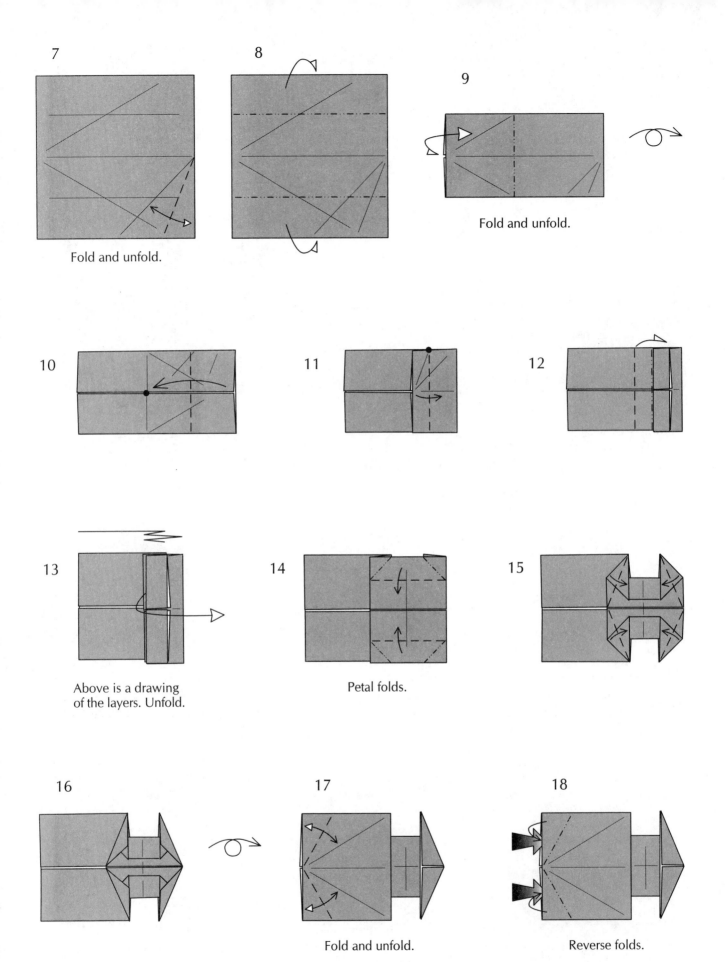

7

Fold and unfold.

8

9

Fold and unfold.

10

11

12

13

Above is a drawing
of the layers. Unfold.

14

Petal folds.

15

16

17

Fold and unfold.

18

Reverse folds.

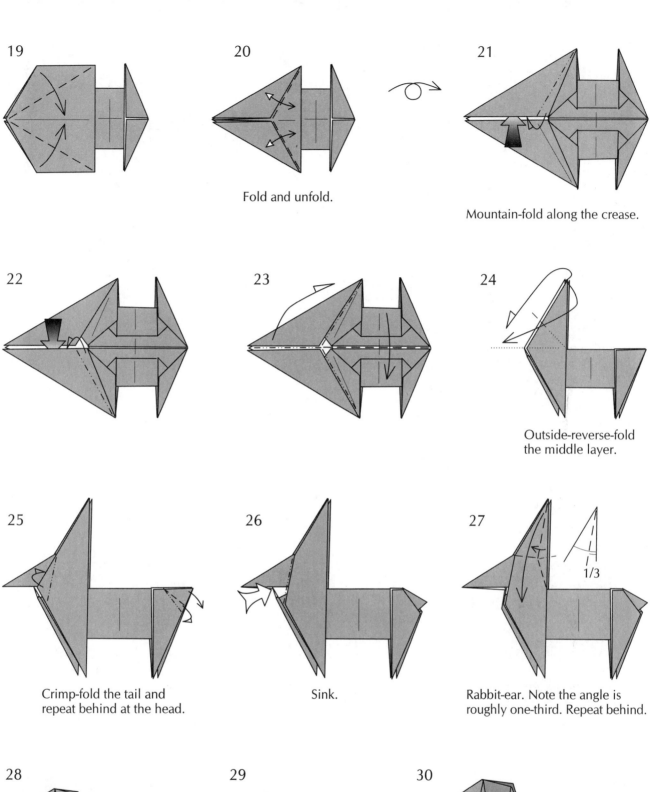

19

20

Fold and unfold.

21

Mountain-fold along the crease.

22

23

24

Outside-reverse-fold
the middle layer.

25

Crimp-fold the tail and
repeat behind at the head.

26

Sink.

27

1/3

Rabbit-ear. Note the angle is
roughly one-third. Repeat behind.

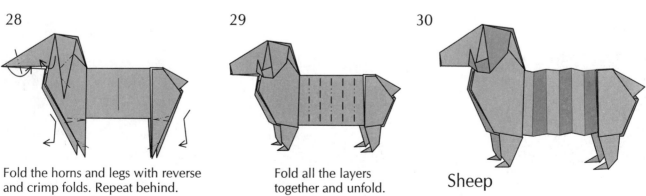

28

Fold the horns and legs with reverse
and crimp folds. Repeat behind.

29

Fold all the layers
together and unfold.

30

Sheep

Cow

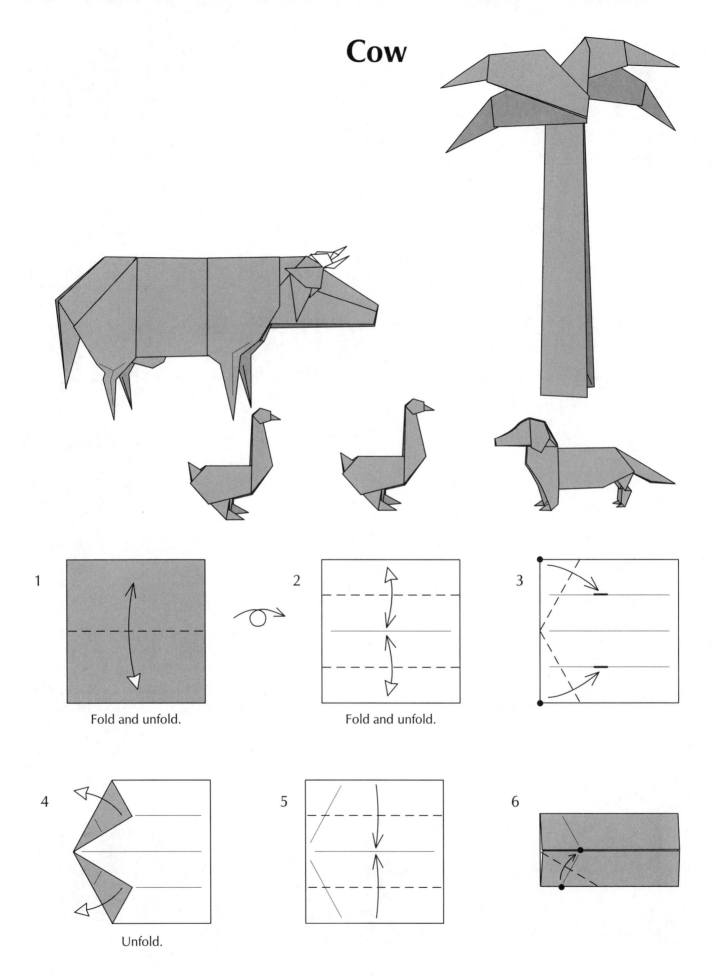

1 Fold and unfold.

2 Fold and unfold.

3

4 Unfold.

5

6

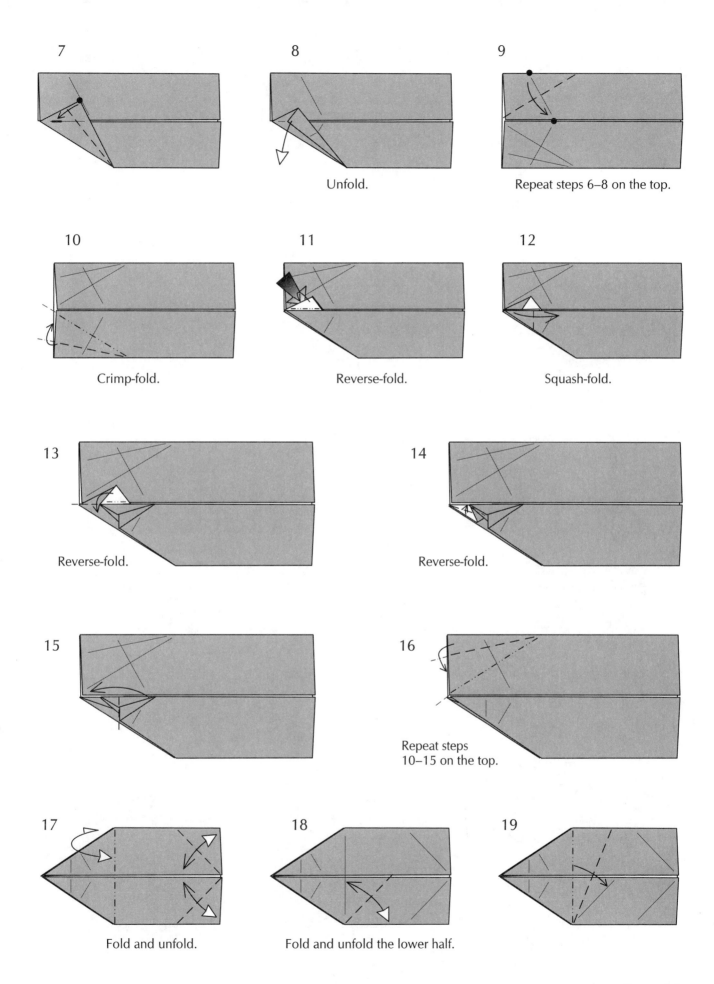

7

8

Unfold.

9

Repeat steps 6–8 on the top.

10

Crimp-fold.

11

Reverse-fold.

12

Squash-fold.

13

Reverse-fold.

14

Reverse-fold.

15

16

Repeat steps
10–15 on the top.

17

Fold and unfold.

18

Fold and unfold the lower half.

19

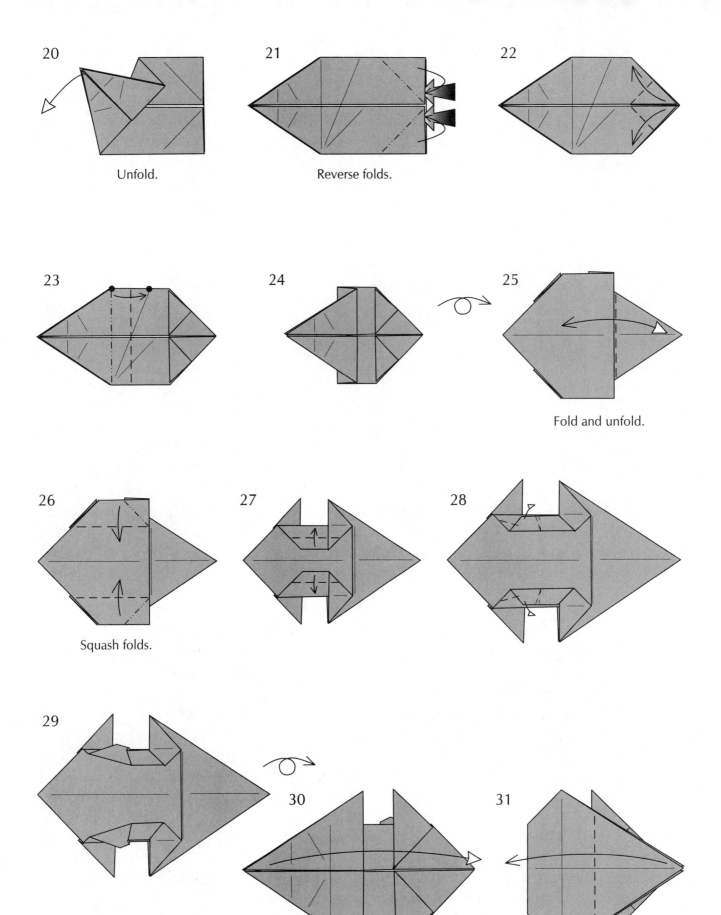

20

Unfold.

21

Reverse folds.

22

23

24

25

Fold and unfold.

26

Squash folds.

27

28

29

30

Unfold.

31

40 *Christmas Origami*

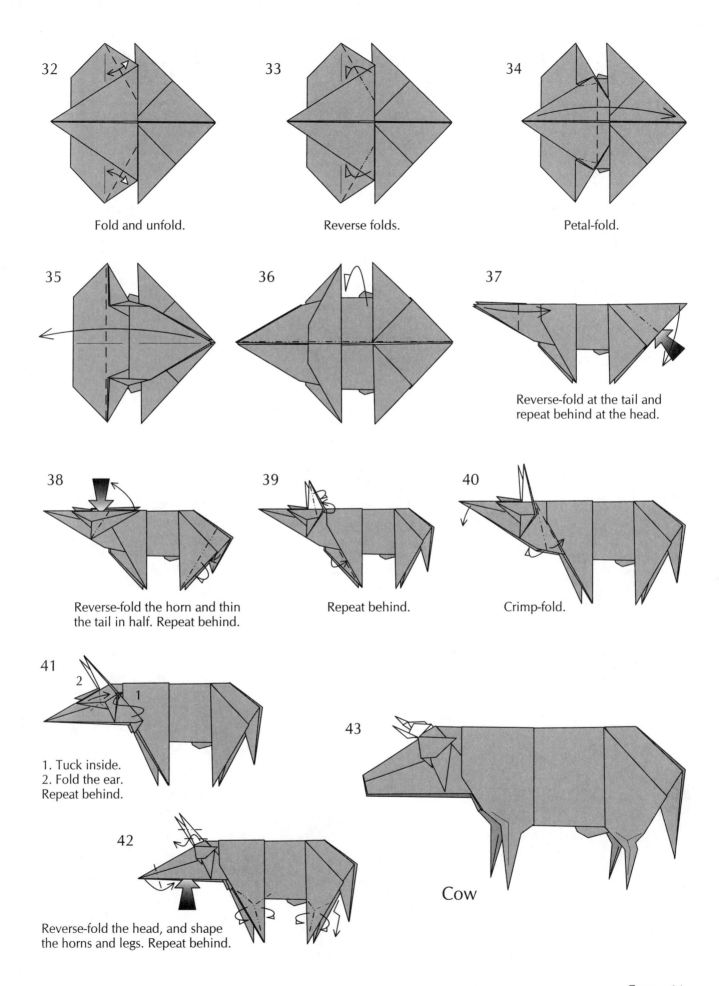

32 Fold and unfold.

33 Reverse folds.

34 Petal-fold.

35

36

37 Reverse-fold at the tail and repeat behind at the head.

38 Reverse-fold the horn and thin the tail in half. Repeat behind.

39 Repeat behind.

40 Crimp-fold.

41
1. Tuck inside.
2. Fold the ear.
Repeat behind.

42 Reverse-fold the head, and shape the horns and legs. Repeat behind.

43

Cow

The Twelve Days of Christmas

On the twelfth day of Christmas,
my true love sent to me

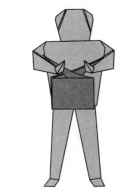

Twelve drummers drumming,

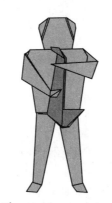

Eleven pipers piping,

Ten lords a-leaping,

Nine ladies dancing,

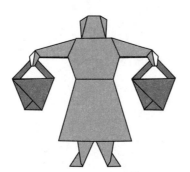

Eight maids a-milking,

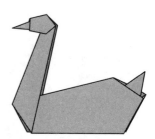

Seven swans a-swimming,

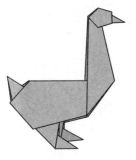

Six geese a-laying,

Five golden rings,

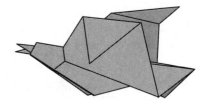

Four calling birds,

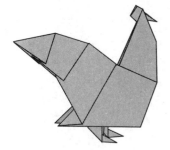

Three French hens,

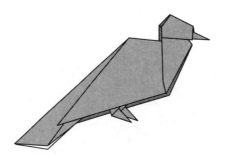

Two turtle doves,

And a partridge in a pear tree.

Partridge

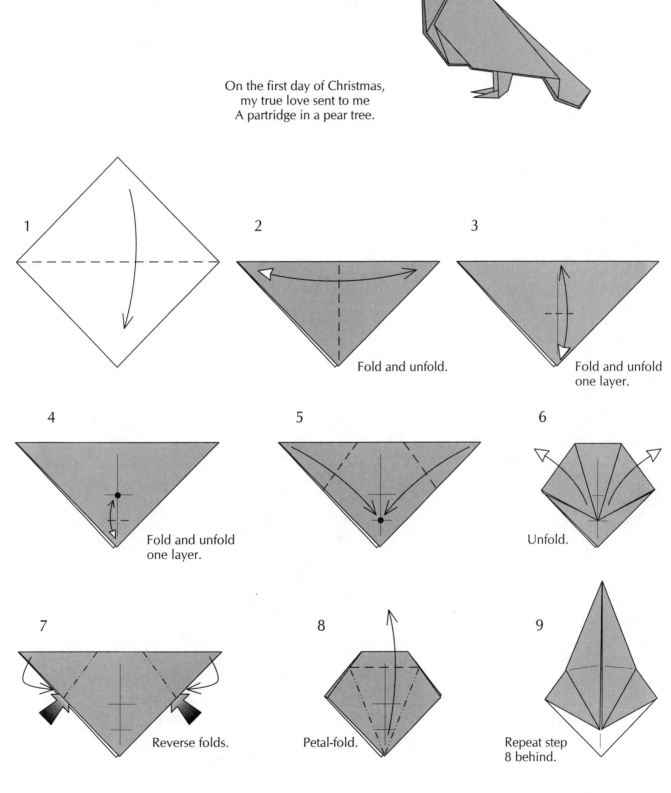

On the first day of Christmas,
my true love sent to me
A partridge in a pear tree.

1

2

Fold and unfold.

3

Fold and unfold
one layer.

4

Fold and unfold
one layer.

5

6

Unfold.

7

Reverse folds.

8

Petal-fold.

9

Repeat step
8 behind.

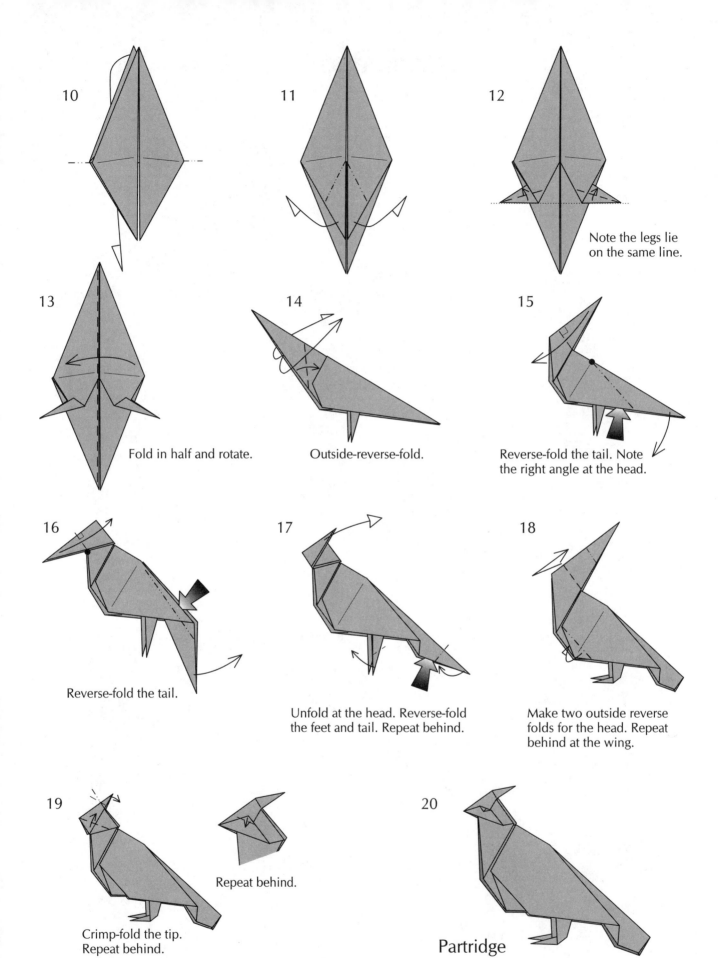

10

11

12

Note the legs lie
on the same line.

13

Fold in half and rotate.

14

Outside-reverse-fold.

15

Reverse-fold the tail. Note
the right angle at the head.

16

Reverse-fold the tail.

17

Unfold at the head. Reverse-fold
the feet and tail. Repeat behind.

18

Make two outside reverse
folds for the head. Repeat
behind at the wing.

19

Crimp-fold the tip.
Repeat behind.

Repeat behind.

20

Partridge

Turtle Dove

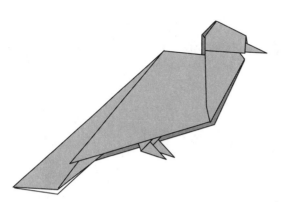

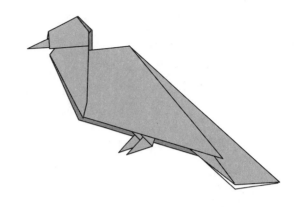

On the second day of Christmas,
my true love sent to me
Two turtle doves,
And a partridge in a pear tree.

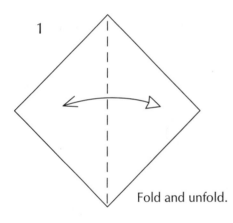

1

Fold and unfold.

2

Fold and unfold
at the corners.

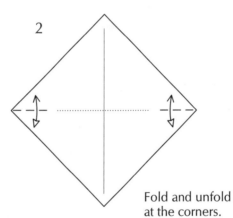

3

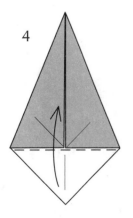

4

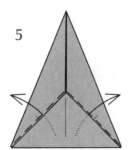

5

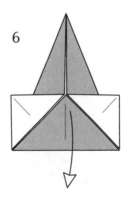

6

Unfold.

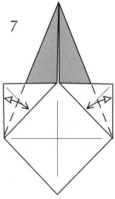

7

Fold and unfold.

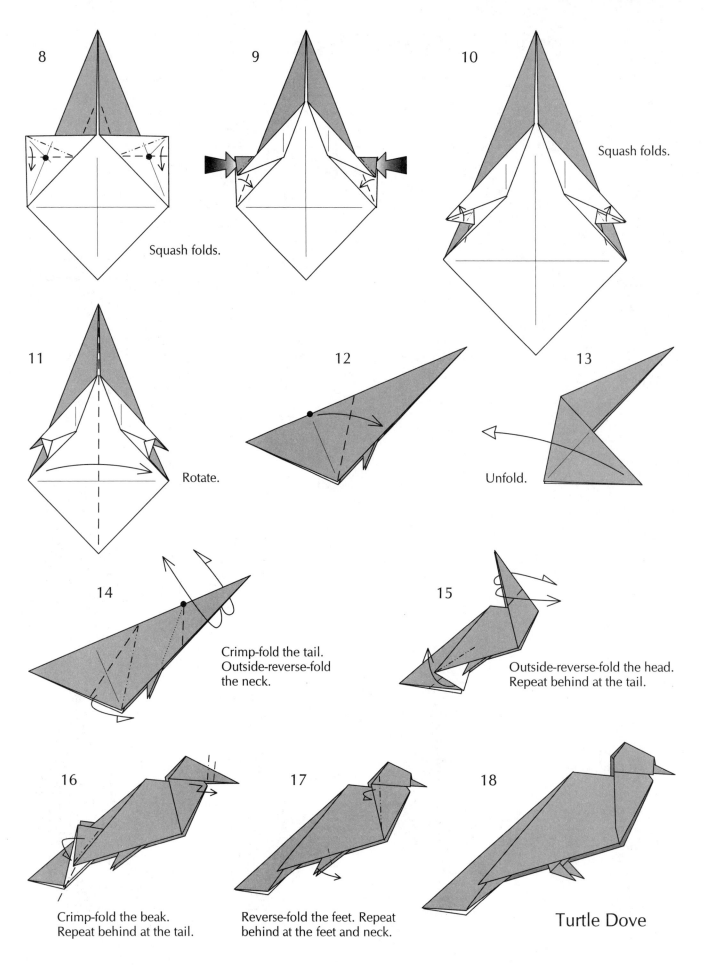

8

Squash folds.

9

Squash folds.

10

Squash folds.

11

Rotate.

12

13

Unfold.

14

Crimp-fold the tail.
Outside-reverse-fold
the neck.

15

Outside-reverse-fold the head.
Repeat behind at the tail.

16

Crimp-fold the beak.
Repeat behind at the tail.

17

Reverse-fold the feet. Repeat
behind at the feet and neck.

18

Turtle Dove

French Hen

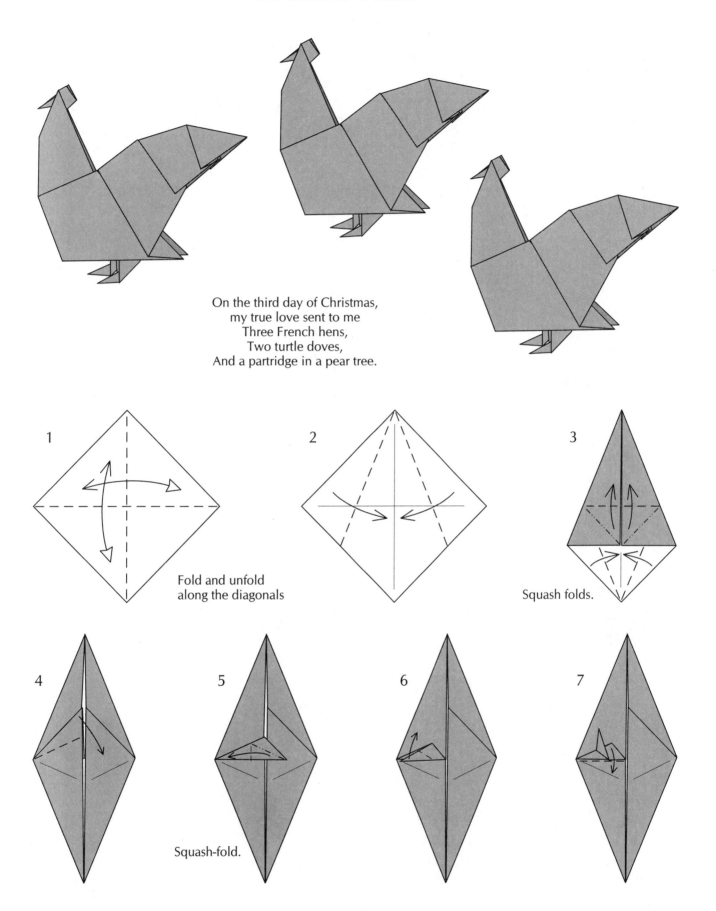

On the third day of Christmas,
my true love sent to me
Three French hens,
Two turtle doves,
And a partridge in a pear tree.

1

Fold and unfold
along the diagonals

2

3

Squash folds.

4

5

Squash-fold.

6

7

8

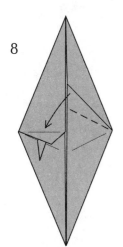

Repeat steps 4–7
on the right.

9

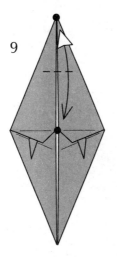

Fold and unfold.

10

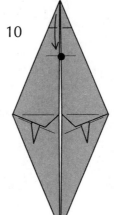

11

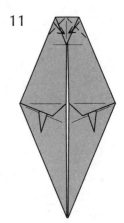

12

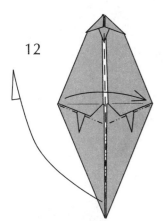

Lift the bottom up
while folding in half.

13

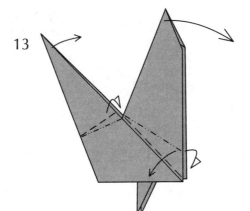

Crimp-fold inside for the neck and
crimp-fold outside for the tail.

14

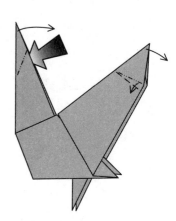

Reverse-fold at the head
and crimp-fold at the tail.

15

Reverse-fold at the head. Reverse-fold
the feet. Crimp-fold the tail.

16

French Hen

Calling Bird

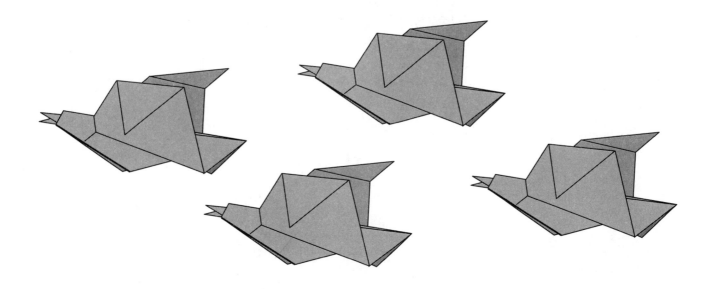

On the fourth day of Christmas,
my true love sent to me
Four calling birds,
Three French hens,
Two turtle doves,
And a partridge in a pear tree.

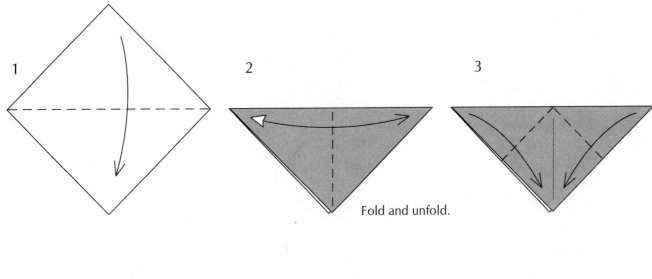

1

2

Fold and unfold.

3

4

5

Lift the corners from behind.

6

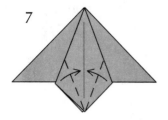

7

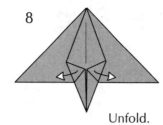

8

Unfold.

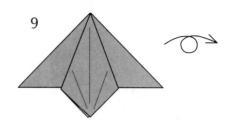

9

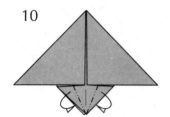

10

Fold inside.

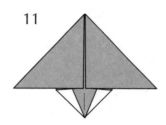

11

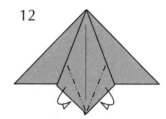

12

Reverse-fold the paper inside.

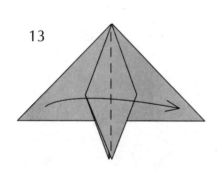

13

Fold in half and rotate.

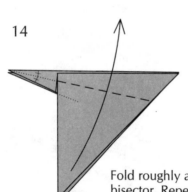

14

Fold roughly along the bisector. Repeat behind.

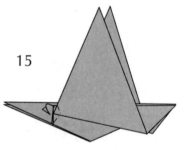

15

Fold behind. Repeat behind.

16

Crimp-fold the beak. Repeat behind at the wing.

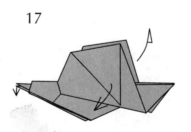

17

Spread the wings and beak.

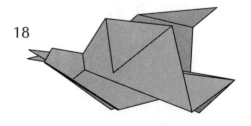

18

Calling Bird

Golden Ring

On the fifth day of Christmas,
my true love sent to me
Five golden rings,
Four calling birds,
Three French hens,
Two turtle doves,
And a partridge in a pear tree.

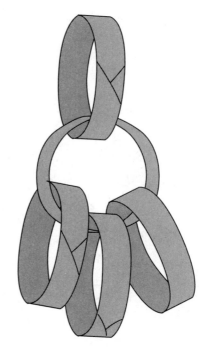

1

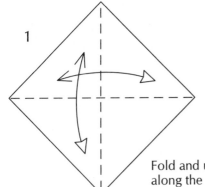

2

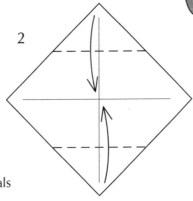

Fold and unfold
along the diagonals

3

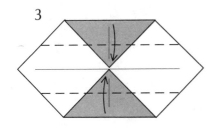

4

1/3

5

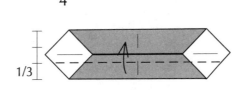

6

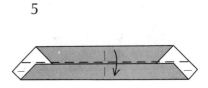

7

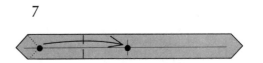

8

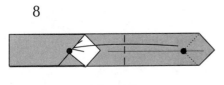

Tuck inside.

9

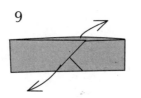

Make the ring round.

10

Golden Ring

Goose

On the sixth day of Christmas,
my true love sent to me
Six geese a-laying,
Five golden rings,
Four calling birds,
Three French hens,
Two turtle doves,
And a partridge in a pear tree.

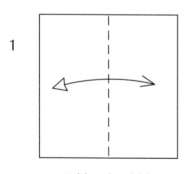

1

Fold and unfold.

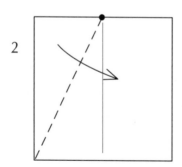

2

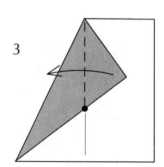

3

4

Repeat steps 2–3 on the right.

5

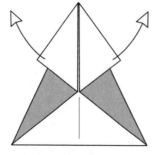

Unfold.

6

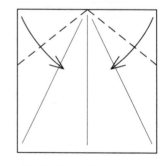

Fold along the creases.

7

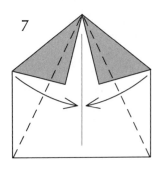

8

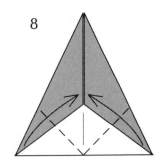

9

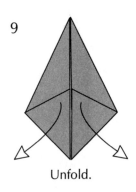

Unfold.

10

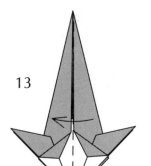

11

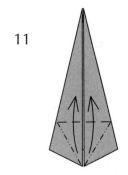

Squash folds.

12

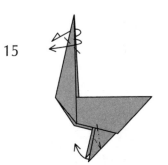

Squash folds.

13

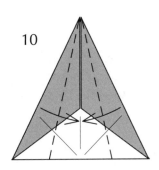

Fold in half and rotate.

14

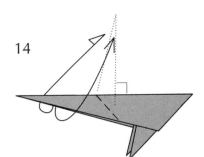

Outside-reverse-fold
at a right angle.

15

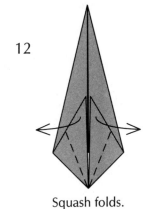

Outside-reverse-fold the head.
Crimp-fold the feet. Repeat behind.

16

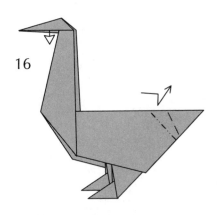

Pull out at the head and repeat
behind. Crimp-fold the tail.

17

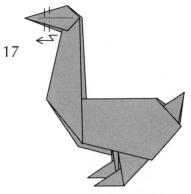

Crimp-fold the beak.

18

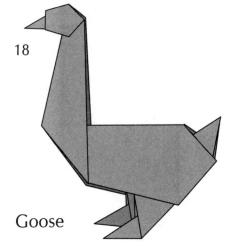

Goose

Goose 53

Swan

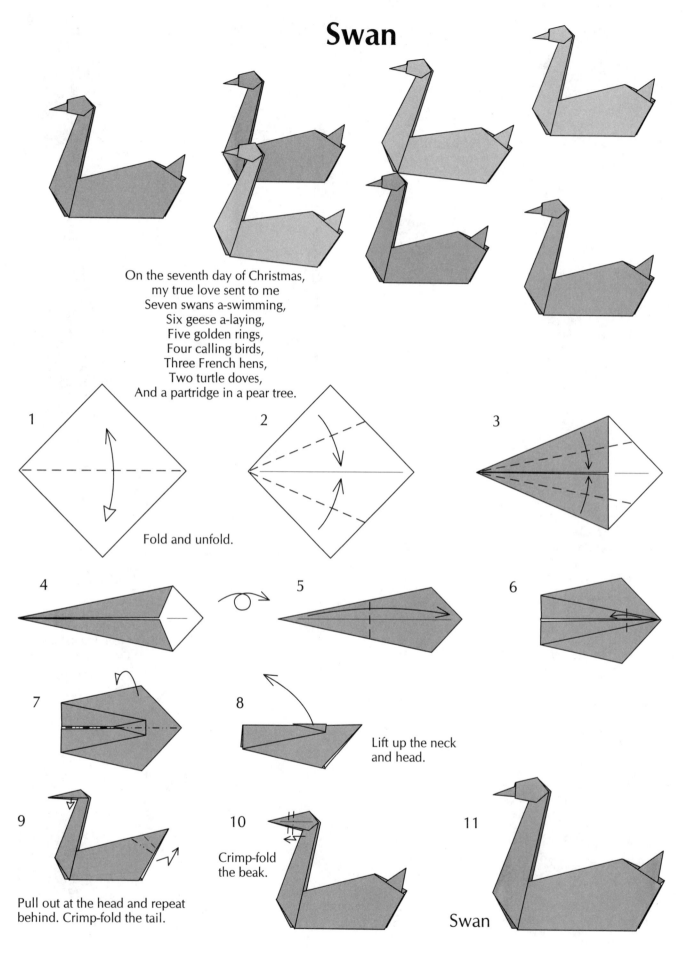

On the seventh day of Christmas,
my true love sent to me
Seven swans a-swimming,
Six geese a-laying,
Five golden rings,
Four calling birds,
Three French hens,
Two turtle doves,
And a partridge in a pear tree.

1

2

Fold and unfold.

3

4

5

6

7

8

Lift up the neck
and head.

9

Pull out at the head and repeat
behind. Crimp-fold the tail.

10

Crimp-fold
the beak.

11

Swan

Maids a-Milking

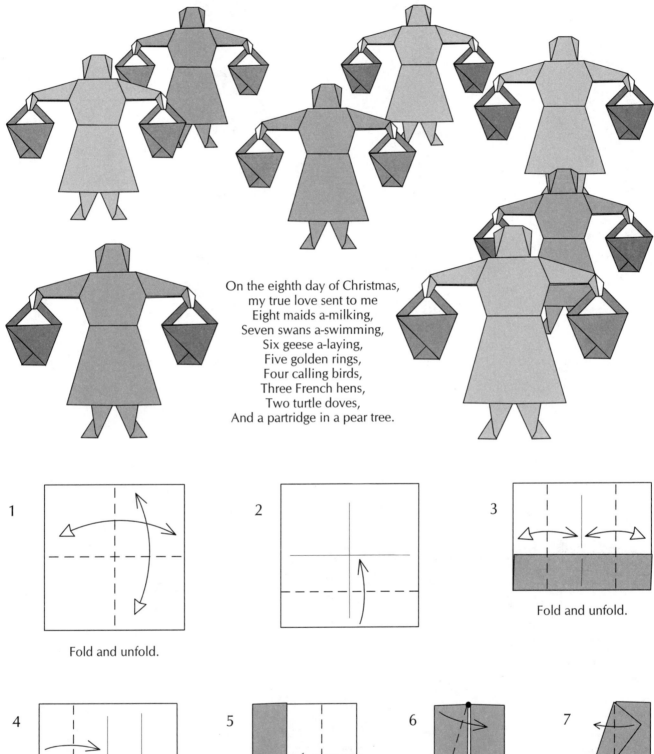

On the eighth day of Christmas,
my true love sent to me
Eight maids a-milking,
Seven swans a-swimming,
Six geese a-laying,
Five golden rings,
Four calling birds,
Three French hens,
Two turtle doves,
And a partridge in a pear tree.

1

Fold and unfold.

2

3

Fold and unfold.

4

Squash-fold.

5

Squash-fold.

6

7

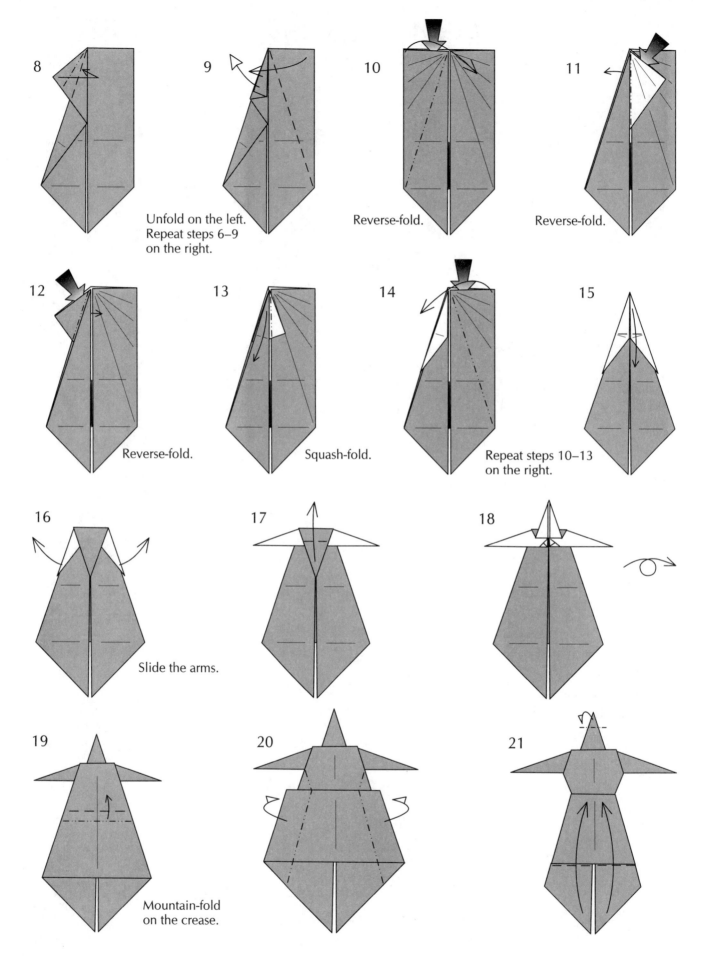

8

9 Unfold on the left.
Repeat steps 6–9
on the right.

10 Reverse-fold.

11 Reverse-fold.

12 Reverse-fold.

13 Squash-fold.

14 Repeat steps 10–13
on the right.

15

16 Slide the arms.

17

18

19 Mountain-fold
on the crease.

20

21

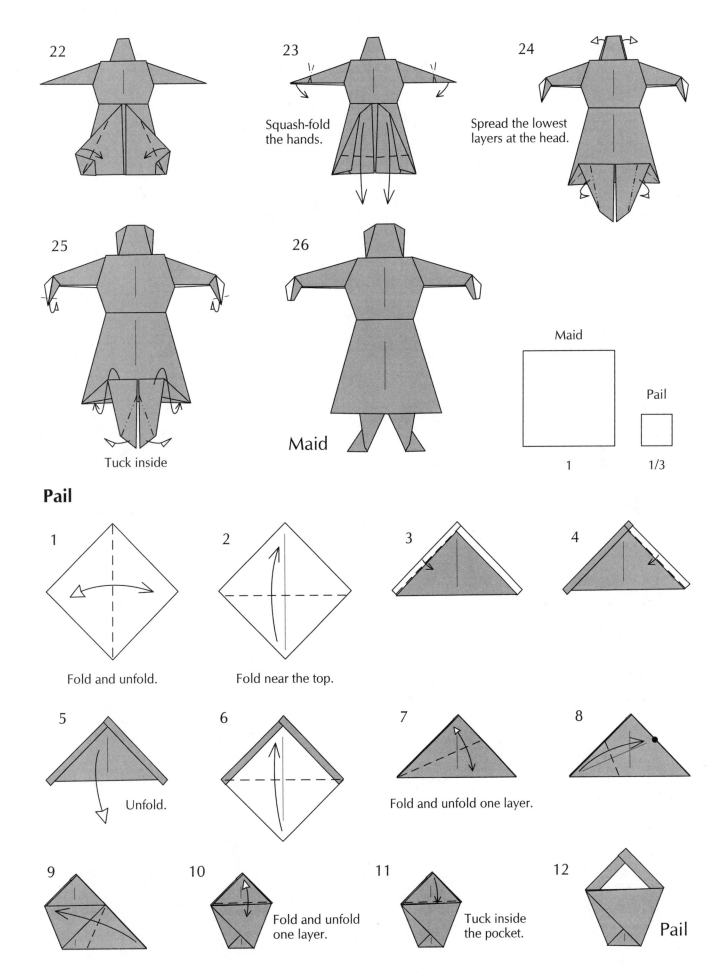

22

23 Squash-fold the hands.

24 Spread the lowest layers at the head.

25 Tuck inside

26 Maid

Maid

1

Pail

1/3

Pail

1 Fold and unfold.

2 Fold near the top.

3

4

5 Unfold.

6

7 Fold and unfold one layer.

8

9

10 Fold and unfold one layer.

11 Tuck inside the pocket.

12 Pail

Ladies Dancing

On the ninth day of Christmas,
my true love sent to me
Nine ladies dancing,
Eight maids a-milking,
Seven swans a-swimming,
Six geese a-laying,
Five golden rings,
Four calling birds,
Three French hens,
Two turtle doves,
And a partridge in a pear tree.

Begin with the Maid, but do not fold the hands.

1

Reverse folds.

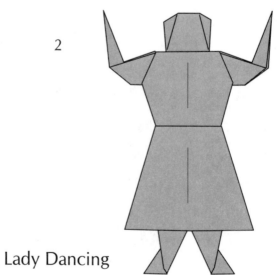

2

Lady Dancing

Lords a-Leaping

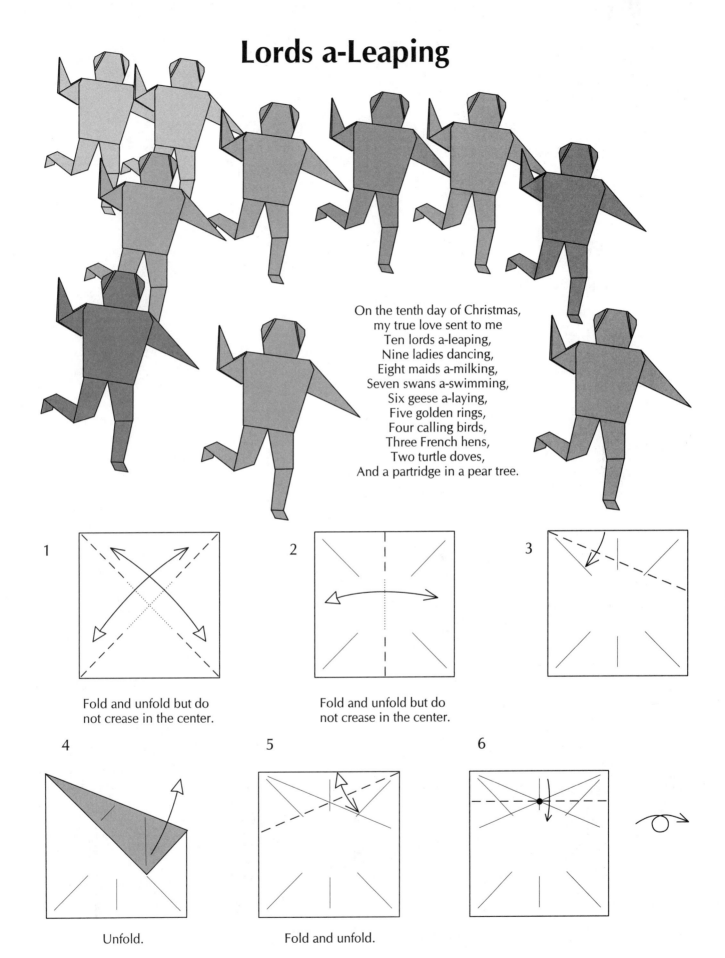

On the tenth day of Christmas,
my true love sent to me
Ten lords a-leaping,
Nine ladies dancing,
Eight maids a-milking,
Seven swans a-swimming,
Six geese a-laying,
Five golden rings,
Four calling birds,
Three French hens,
Two turtle doves,
And a partridge in a pear tree.

1

Fold and unfold but do
not crease in the center.

2

Fold and unfold but do
not crease in the center.

3

4

Unfold.

5

Fold and unfold.

6

7 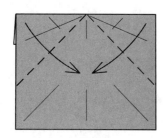 8 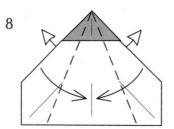 9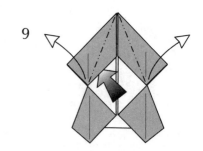

Spread.

10 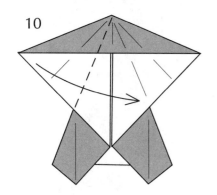 11 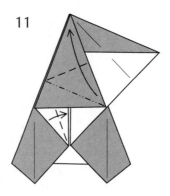 12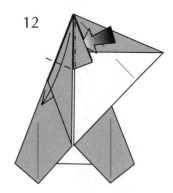

Squash-fold.

Squash-fold.

13 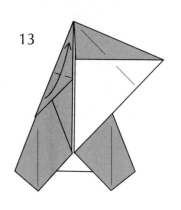 14 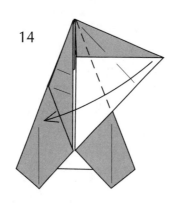 15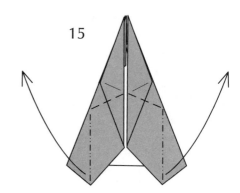

Repeat steps 10–13
on the right.

Petal-fold.

16 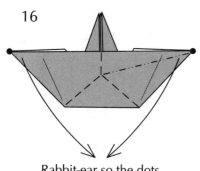 17 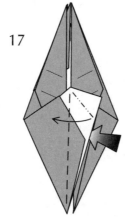 18 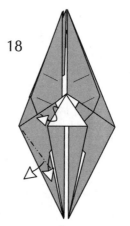 19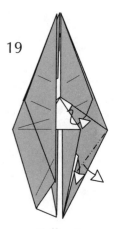

Rabbit-ear so the dots
meet at the bottom.

Squash-fold.

Pull out.

Pull out.

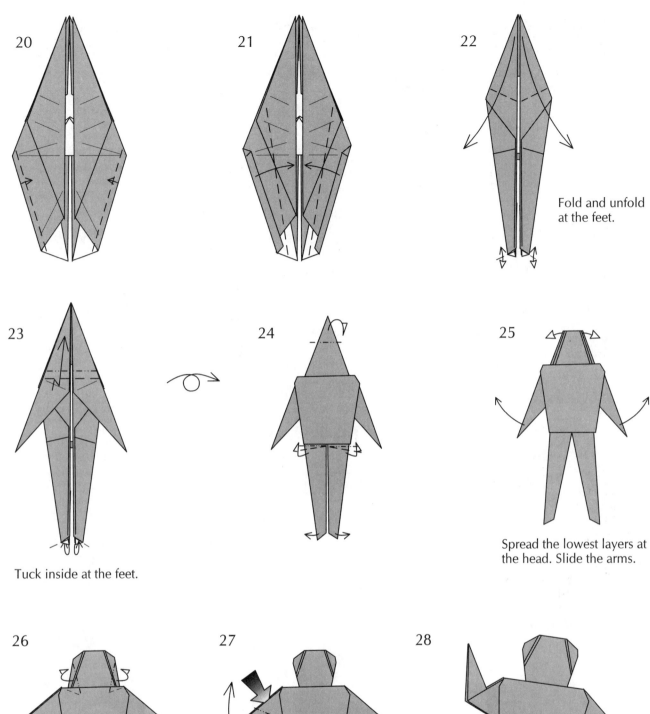

20

21

22

Fold and unfold at the feet.

23

Tuck inside at the feet.

24

25

Spread the lowest layers at the head. Slide the arms.

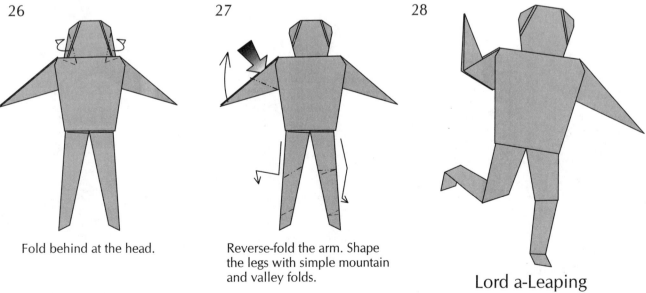

26

Fold behind at the head.

27

Reverse-fold the arm. Shape the legs with simple mountain and valley folds.

28

Lord a-Leaping

Pipers Piping

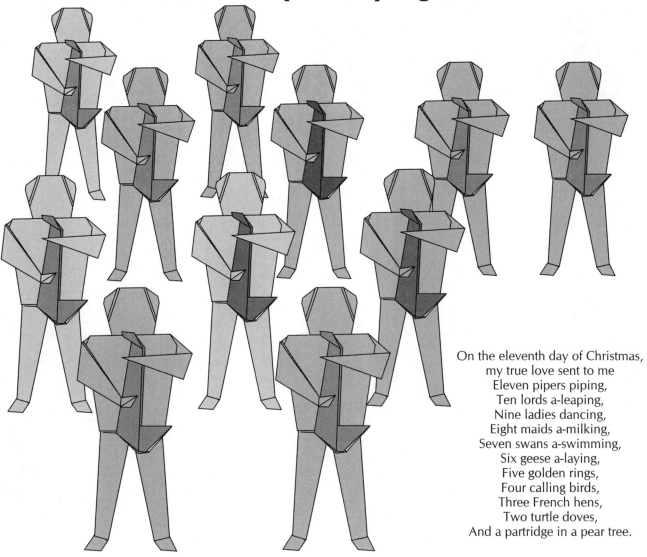

On the eleventh day of Christmas,
my true love sent to me
Eleven pipers piping,
Ten lords a-leaping,
Nine ladies dancing,
Eight maids a-milking,
Seven swans a-swimming,
Six geese a-laying,
Five golden rings,
Four calling birds,
Three French hens,
Two turtle doves,
And a partridge in a pear tree.

Begin with step 27 of the Lord a-Leaping.

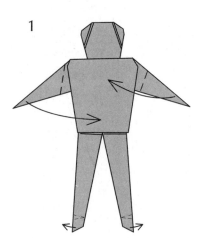

1

Shape the feet with simple
mountain and valley folds.

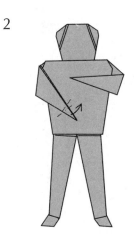

2

Squash-fold.

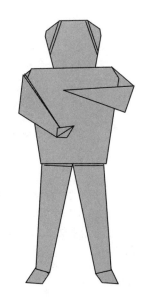

3

Piper Piping

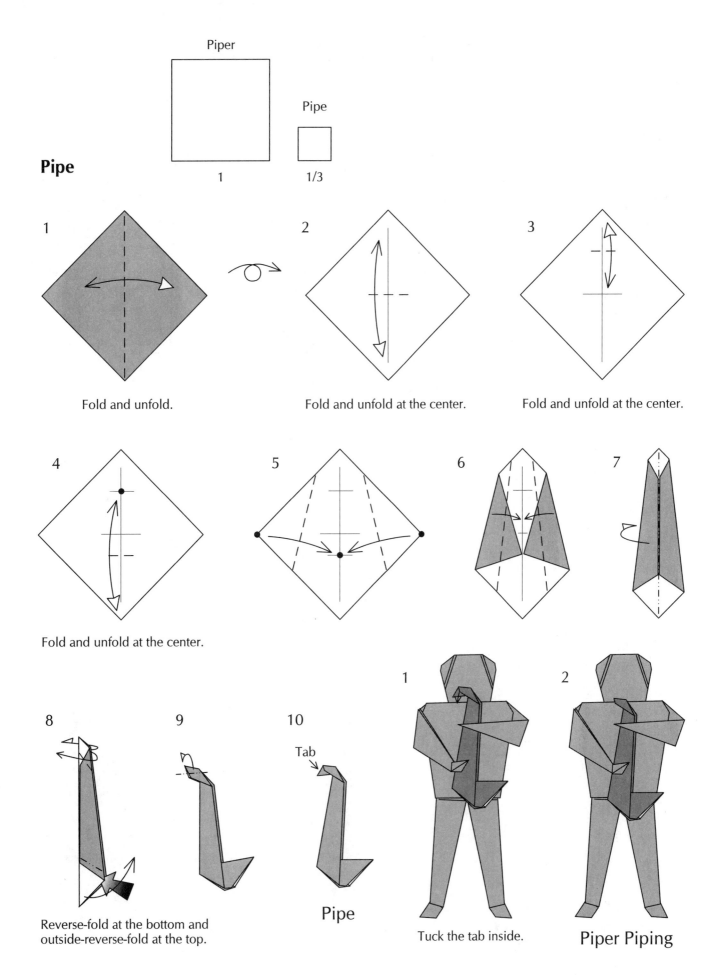

Piper

Pipe

1

1/3

Pipe

1 Fold and unfold.

2 Fold and unfold at the center.

3 Fold and unfold at the center.

4 Fold and unfold at the center.

5

6

7

8 Reverse-fold at the bottom and outside-reverse-fold at the top.

9

10 Tab

Pipe

1 Tuck the tab inside.

2 Piper Piping

Drummers Drumming

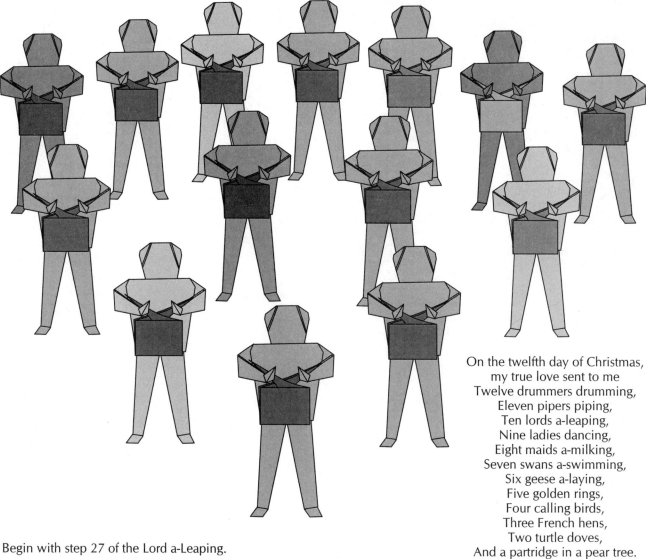

On the twelfth day of Christmas,
my true love sent to me
Twelve drummers drumming,
Eleven pipers piping,
Ten lords a-leaping,
Nine ladies dancing,
Eight maids a-milking,
Seven swans a-swimming,
Six geese a-laying,
Five golden rings,
Four calling birds,
Three French hens,
Two turtle doves,
And a partridge in a pear tree.

Begin with step 27 of the Lord a-Leaping.

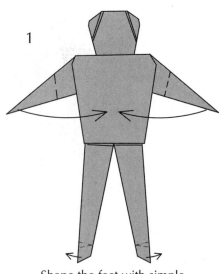

1

Shape the feet with simple
mountain and valley folds.

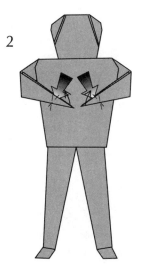

2

Squash folds.

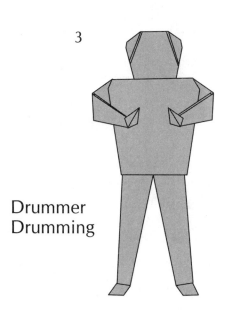

3

Drummer
Drumming

Drum

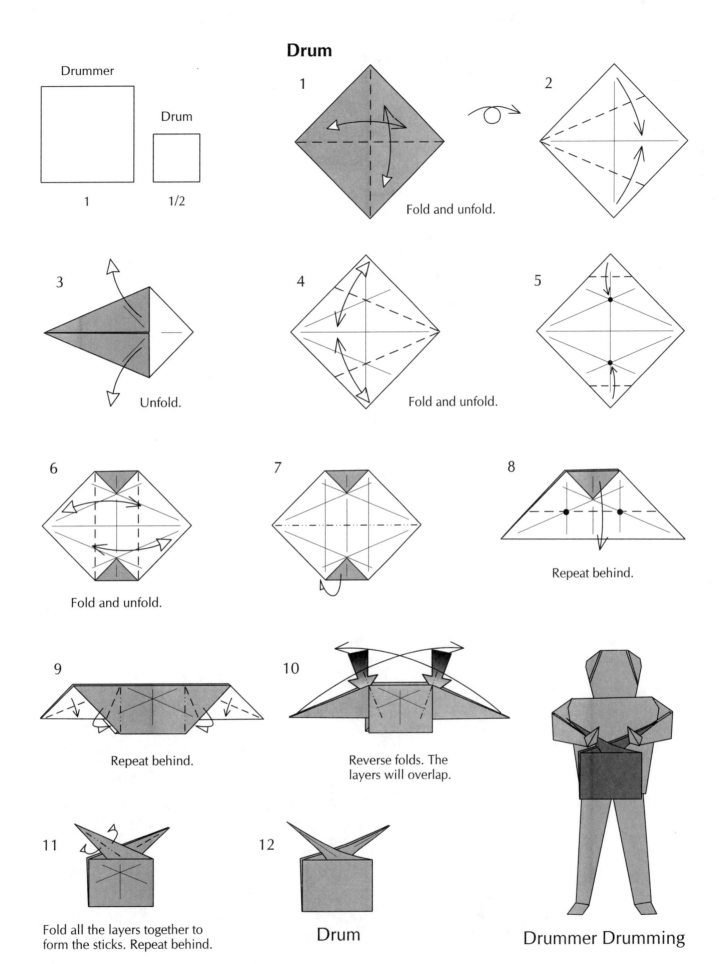

Drummer

Drum

1   1/2

1 Fold and unfold.

2

3 Unfold.

4 Fold and unfold.

5

6 Fold and unfold.

7

8 Repeat behind.

9 Repeat behind.

10 Reverse folds. The layers will overlap.

11 Fold all the layers together to form the sticks. Repeat behind.

12 Drum

Drummer Drumming

Tree Ornaments and Gifts

Stocking

Jolly old Saint Nicholas,
Lean your ear this way!
Don't you tell a single soul
What I'm going to say;
Christmas Eve is coming soon;
Now, you dear old man,
Whisper what you'll bring to me;
Tell me if you can.

When the clock is striking twelve,
When I'm fast asleep,
Down the chimney broad and black,
With your pack you'll creep;
All the stockings you will find
Hanging in a row;
Mine will be the shortest one,
You'll be sure to know.

Johnny wants a pair of skates;
Susy wants a dolly;
Nellie wants a story book;
She thinks dolls are folly;
As for me, my little brain
Isn't very bright;
Choose for me, old Santa Claus,
What you think is right.

1

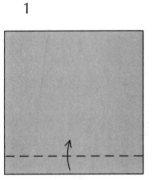

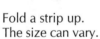

Fold a strip up.
The size can vary.

2

Fold to the right.
The size can vary.

3

4

Fold and unfold.

5

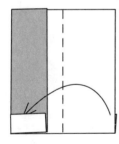

Tuck inside.

6

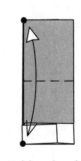

Fold and unfold.

7

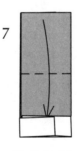

Tuck inside.

8

9

Unfold.

10

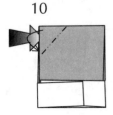

Reverse-fold.

11

Open to make the stocking
three-dimensional. Rotate.

12

Stocking

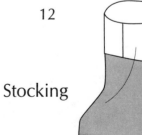

Candy Cane

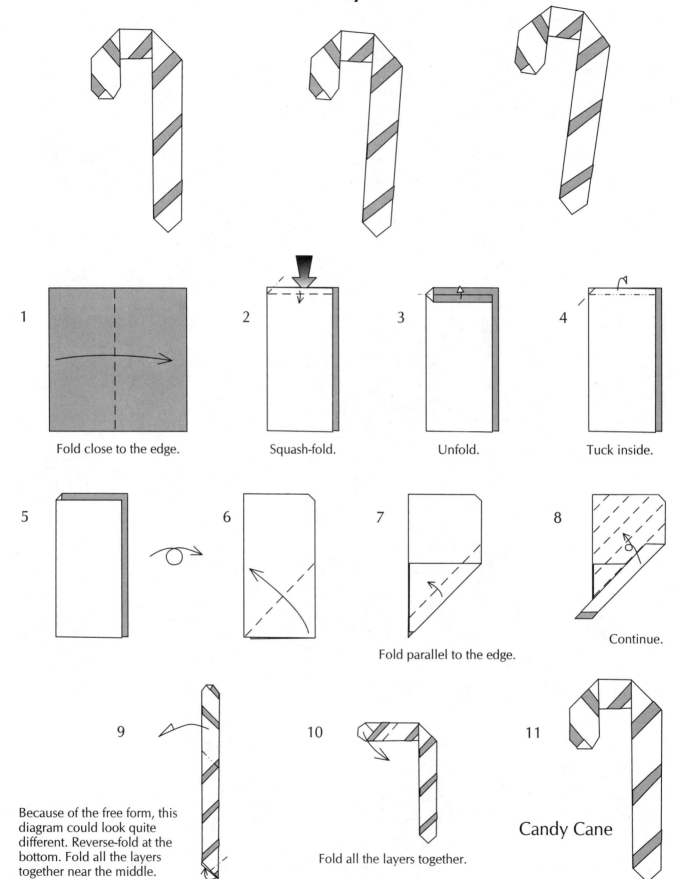

1 Fold close to the edge.

2 Squash-fold.

3 Unfold.

4 Tuck inside.

5

6

7 Fold parallel to the edge.

8 Continue.

9 Because of the free form, this diagram could look quite different. Reverse-fold at the bottom. Fold all the layers together near the middle.

10 Fold all the layers together.

11 Candy Cane

Bell

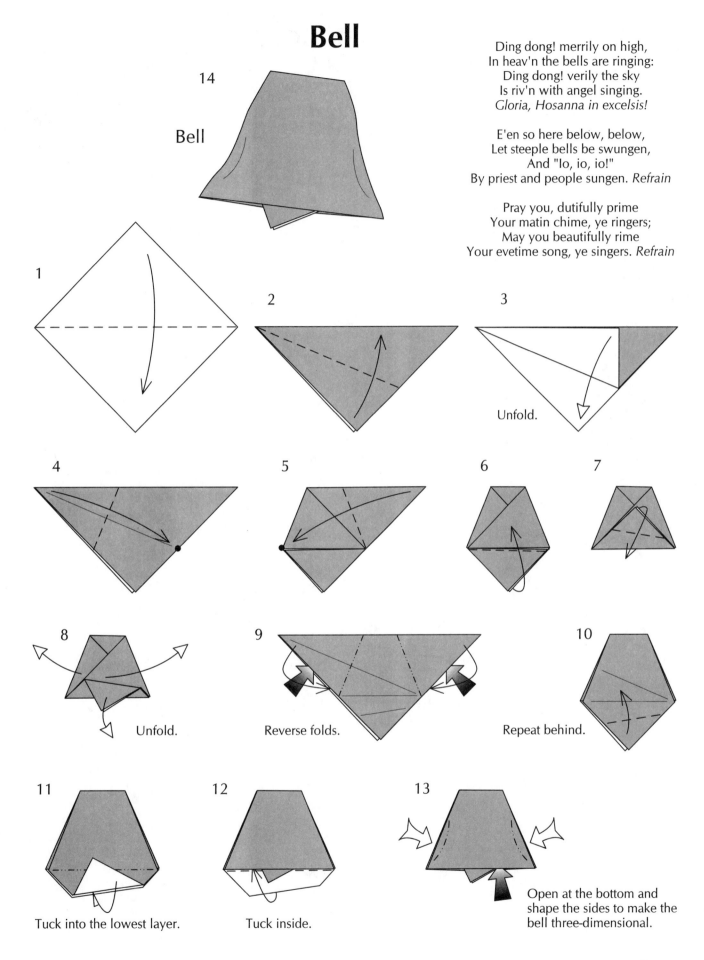

14

Bell

Ding dong! merrily on high,
In heav'n the bells are ringing:
Ding dong! verily the sky
Is riv'n with angel singing.
Gloria, Hosanna in excelsis!

E'en so here below, below,
Let steeple bells be swungen,
And "Io, io, io!"
By priest and people sungen. *Refrain*

Pray you, dutifully prime
Your matin chime, ye ringers;
May you beautifully rime
Your evetime song, ye singers. *Refrain*

1

2

3

Unfold.

4

5

6

7

8

Unfold.

9

Reverse folds.

10

Repeat behind.

11

Tuck into the lowest layer.

12

Tuck inside.

13

Open at the bottom and shape the sides to make the bell three-dimensional.

Candle

O Christmas tree, O Christmas tree,
Thy candles shine out brightly!
Each bough doth hold its tiny light,
That makes each toy to sparkle bright.

O Christmas tree, O Christmas tree,
Thy candles shine out brightly!

1

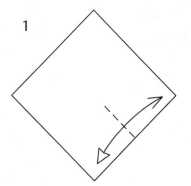

Fold and unfold.

2

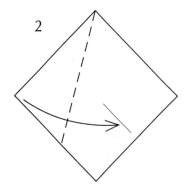

Fold the corner to the line.

3

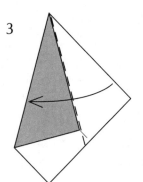

4

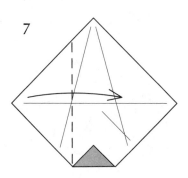

5

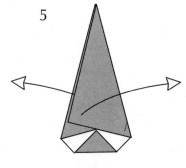

Unfold.

6

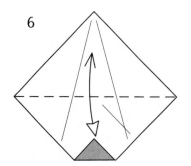

Fold and unfold.

7

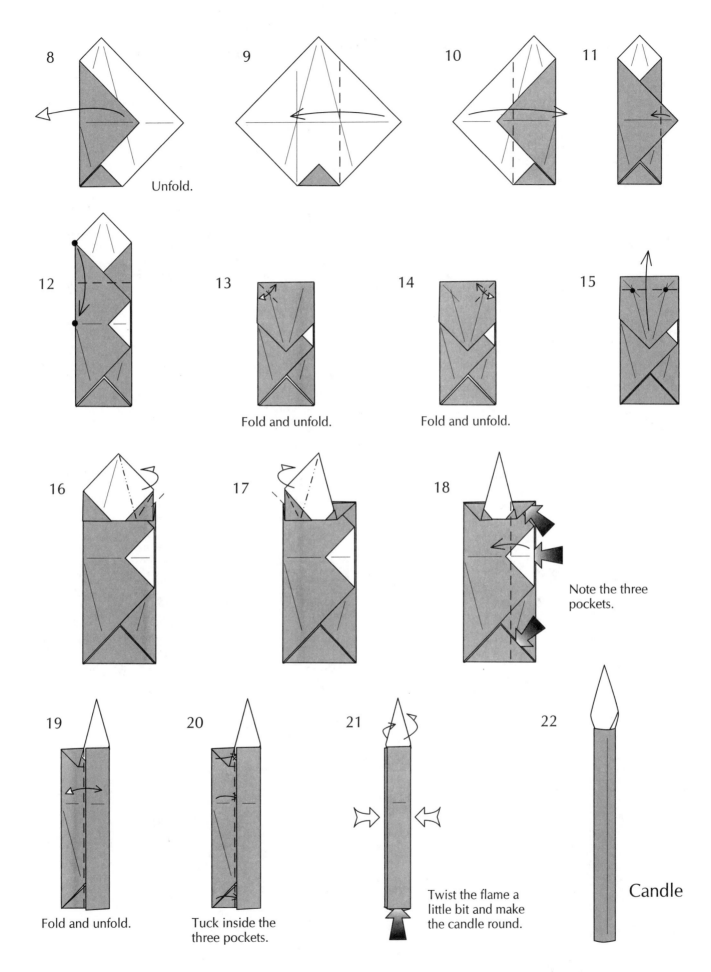

8

9 Unfold.

10

11

12

13 Fold and unfold.

14 Fold and unfold.

15

16

17

18 Note the three pockets.

19 Fold and unfold.

20 Tuck inside the three pockets.

21 Twist the flame a little bit and make the candle round.

22 Candle

Five-Pointed Star

Said the night wind to the little lamb,
"Do you see what I see?
Way up in the sky, little lamb,
Do you see what I see?
A star, a star, dancing in the night
With a tail as big as a kite,
With a tail as big as a kite."

Said the little lamb to the shepherd boy,
"Do you hear what I hear?
Ringing through the sky, shepherd boy,
Do you hear what I hear?
A song, a song high above the trees
With a voice as big as the the sea,
With a voice as big as the the sea."

Said the shepherd boy to the mighty king,
"Do you know what I know?
In your palace warm, mighty king,
Do you know what I know?
A Child, a Child shivers in the cold--
Let us bring him silver and gold,
Let us bring him silver and gold."

Said the king to the people everywhere,
"Listen to what I say!
Pray for peace, people, everywhere,
Listen to what I say!
The Child, the Child sleeping in the night
He will bring us goodness and light,
He will bring us goodness and light."

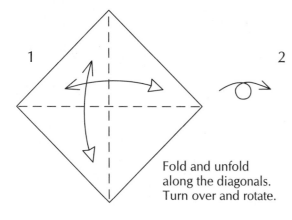

1

Fold and unfold
along the diagonals.
Turn over and rotate.

2

Fold and unfold.

3

Bring the corner to the line
creasing at the bottom.

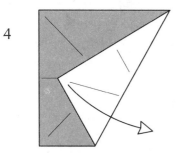

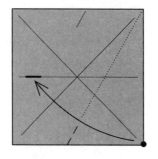

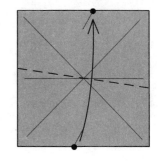

4

Unfold and rotate 180°.

5

Repeat steps 3–4.

6

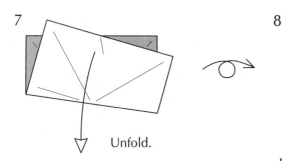

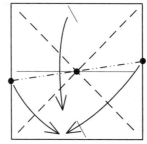

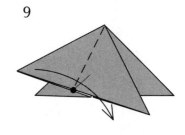

7

Unfold.

8

Push in at the center to collapse
along the creases. This is similar
to the waterbomb base.

9

Turn over and repeat.

10

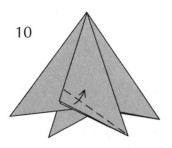

Fold the thin strip up as high as possible. Turn over and repeat.

11

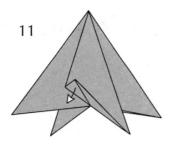

Unfold. Turn over and repeat.

12

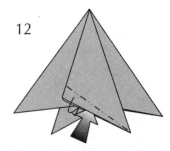

Sink by tucking between the white layers. Turn over and repeat.

13

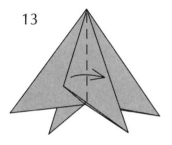

Turn over and repeat.

14

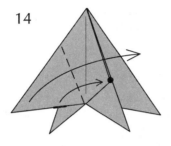

Turn over and repeat.

15

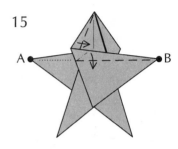

Imagine the line between A and B. Squash-fold along that line. Turn over and repeat.

16

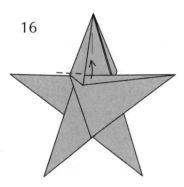

Turn over and repeat.

17

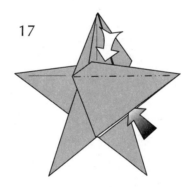

Sink. Turn over and repeat.

18

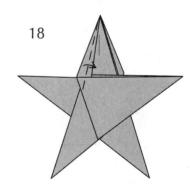

Fold a thin strip. Turn over and repeat.

19

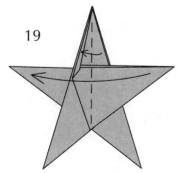

Fold two layers together. Turn over and repeat.

20

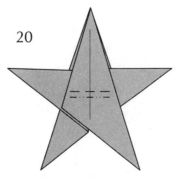

Lightly fold and unfold, without making any crease, in both directions to keep the model together.

21

Five-Pointed Star

Eight-Pointed Star

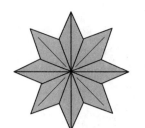

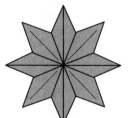

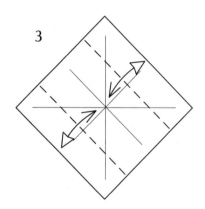

1

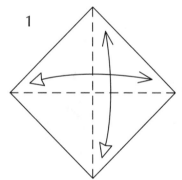

Fold and unfold
along the diagonals.

2

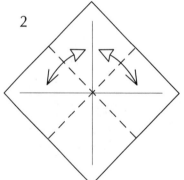

Fold and unfold.

3

Fold and unfold.

4

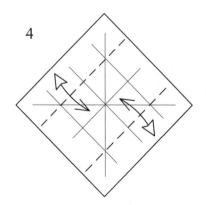

Fold and unfold.

5

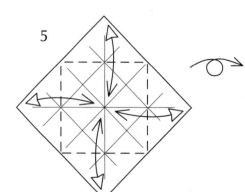

Fold to the center and unfold.

6

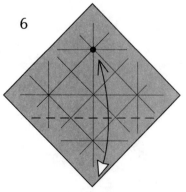

Fold and unfold.

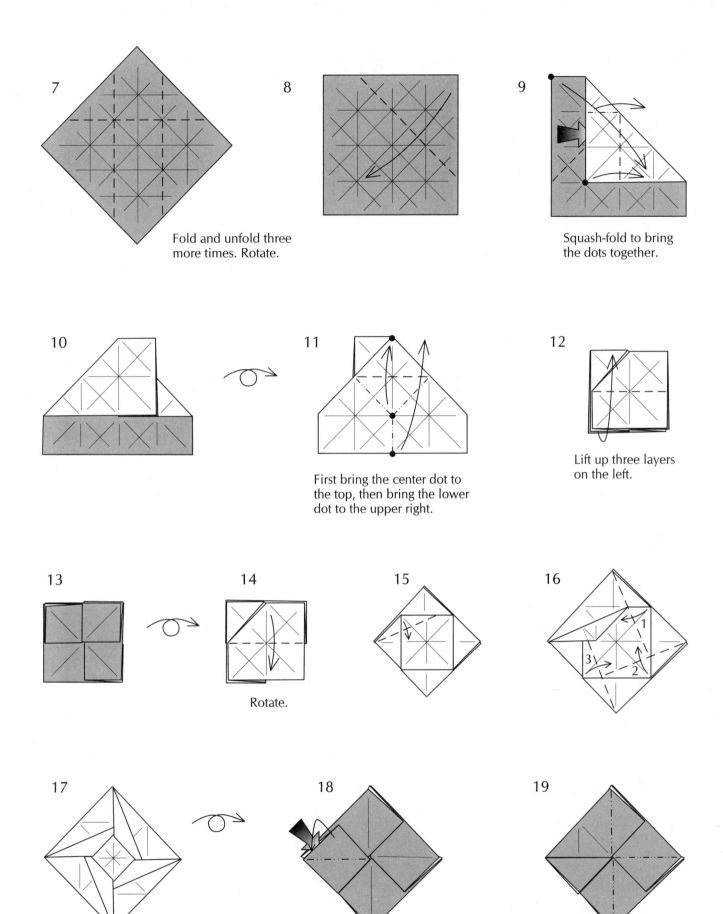

7

8

Fold and unfold three
more times. Rotate.

9

Squash-fold to bring
the dots together.

10

11

First bring the center dot to
the top, then bring the lower
dot to the upper right.

12

Lift up three layers
on the left.

13

14

Rotate.

15

16

17

18

Reverse-fold.

19

Make three more
reverse folds.

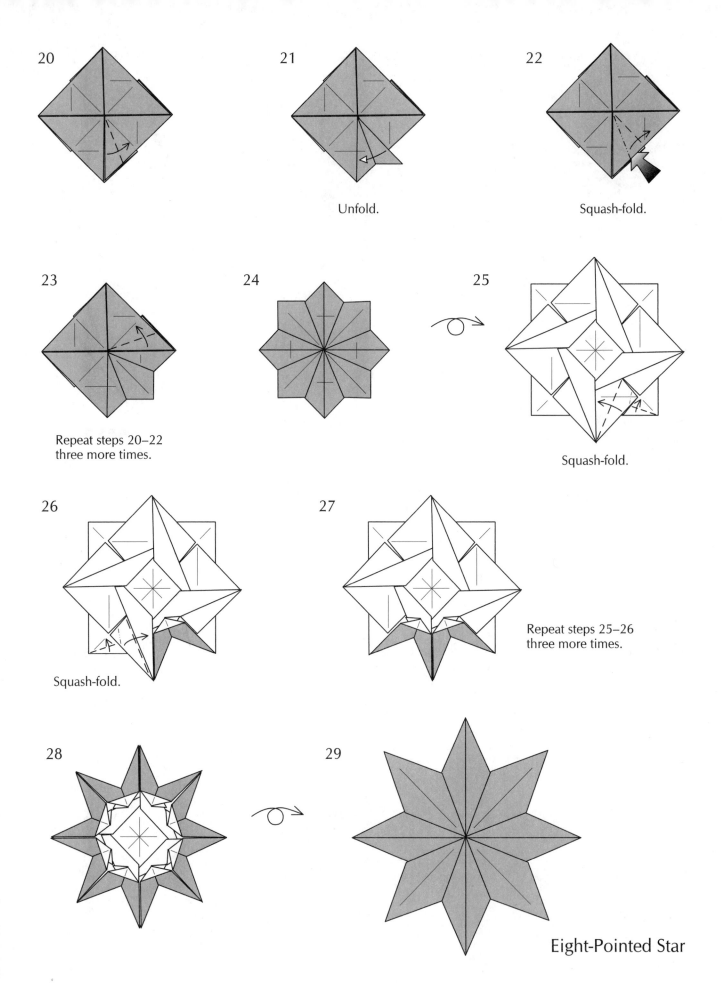

20

21

Unfold.

22

Squash-fold.

23

Repeat steps 20–22
three more times.

24

25

Squash-fold.

26

Squash-fold.

27

Repeat steps 25–26
three more times.

28

29

Eight-Pointed Star

Angel

Angels we have heard on high,
Singing sweetly through the night,
And the mountains in reply
Echoing their brave delight.
Gloria in excelsis Deo.
Gloria in excelsis Deo.

Shepherds, why this jubilee?
Why these songs of happy cheer?
What great brightness did you see?
What glad tiding did you hear? *Refrain*

Come to Bethlehem and see
Him whose birth the angels sing;
Come, adore on bended knee
Christ, the Lord, the new-born King. *Refrain*

See him in a manger laid
Whom the angels praise above;
Mary, Joseph, lend your aid,
While we raise our hearts in love. *Refrain*

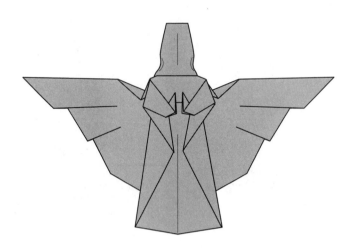

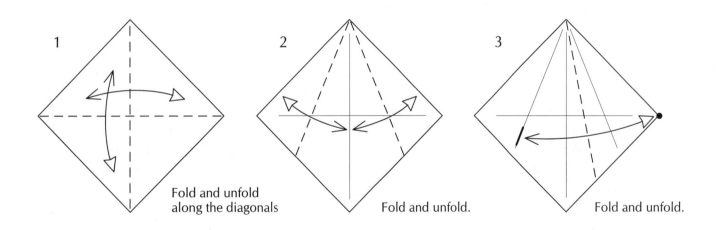

1

Fold and unfold
along the diagonals

2

Fold and unfold.

3

Fold and unfold.

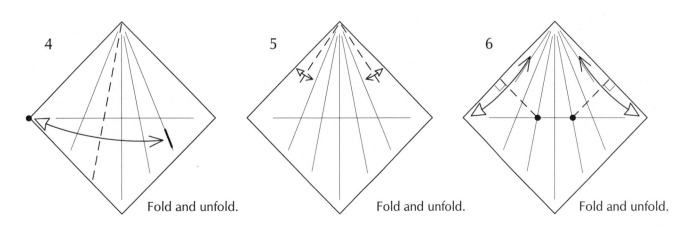

4

Fold and unfold.

5

Fold and unfold.

6

Fold and unfold.

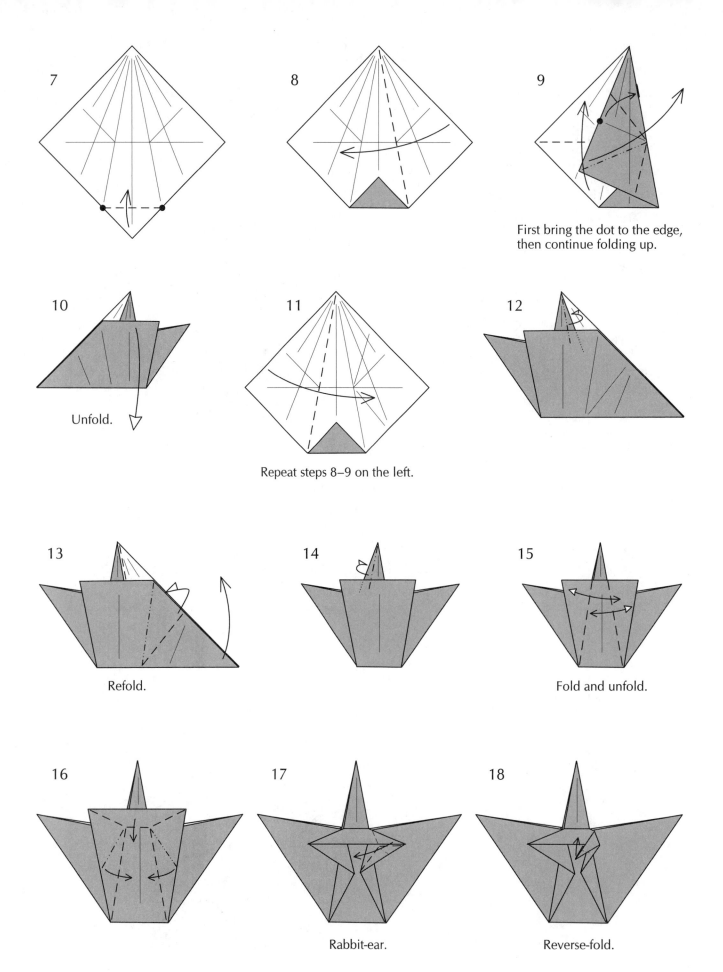

7

8

9

First bring the dot to the edge,
then continue folding up.

10

Unfold.

11

Repeat steps 8–9 on the left.

12

13

Refold.

14

15

Fold and unfold.

16

17

Rabbit-ear.

18

Reverse-fold.

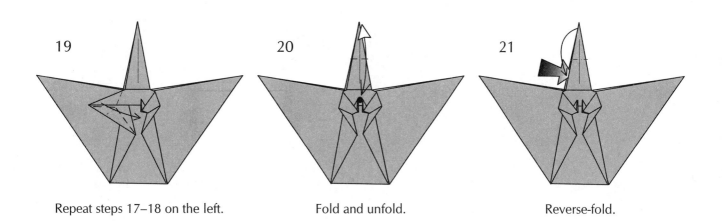

19 Repeat steps 17–18 on the left.

20 Fold and unfold.

21 Reverse-fold.

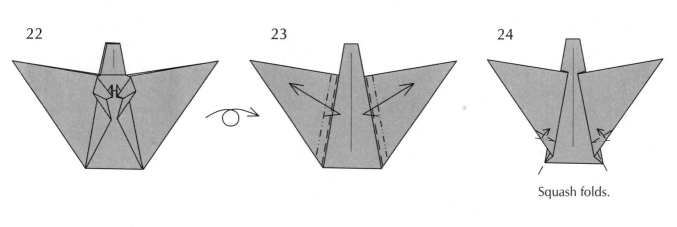

22

23

24 Squash folds.

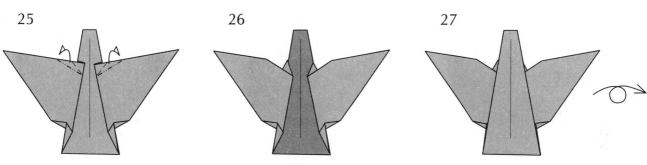

25

26

27

Bring the dark paper to the front.

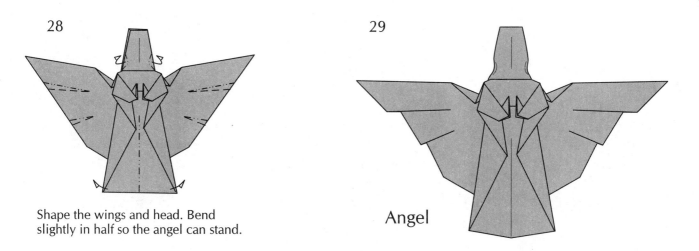

28 Shape the wings and head. Bend slightly in half so the angel can stand.

29 Angel

Nutcracker

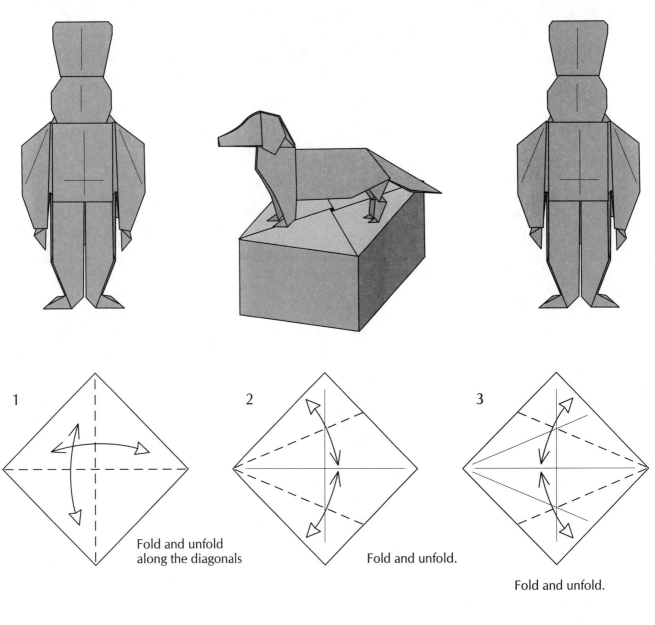

1
Fold and unfold
along the diagonals

2
Fold and unfold.

3
Fold and unfold.

4

5
Fold and unfold the lower half.

6
Fold and unfold the lower half.

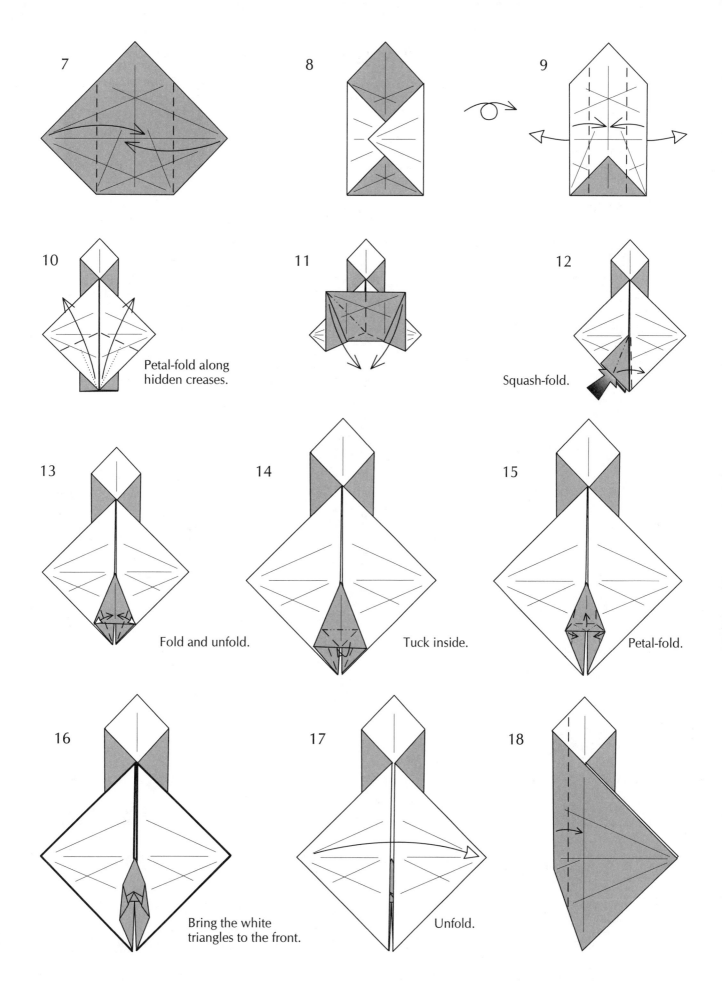

7

8

9

10

Petal-fold along hidden creases.

11

12

Squash-fold.

13

Fold and unfold.

14

Tuck inside.

15

Petal-fold.

16

Bring the white triangles to the front.

17

Unfold.

18

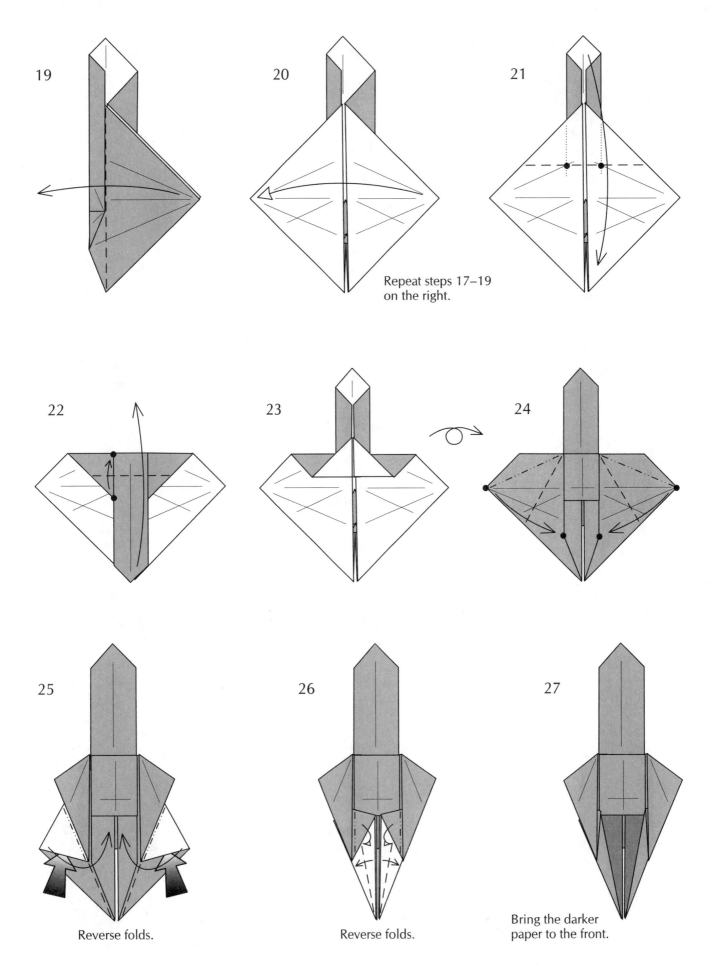

19

20

Repeat steps 17–19
on the right.

21

22

23

24

25

Reverse folds.

26

Reverse folds.

27

Bring the darker
paper to the front.

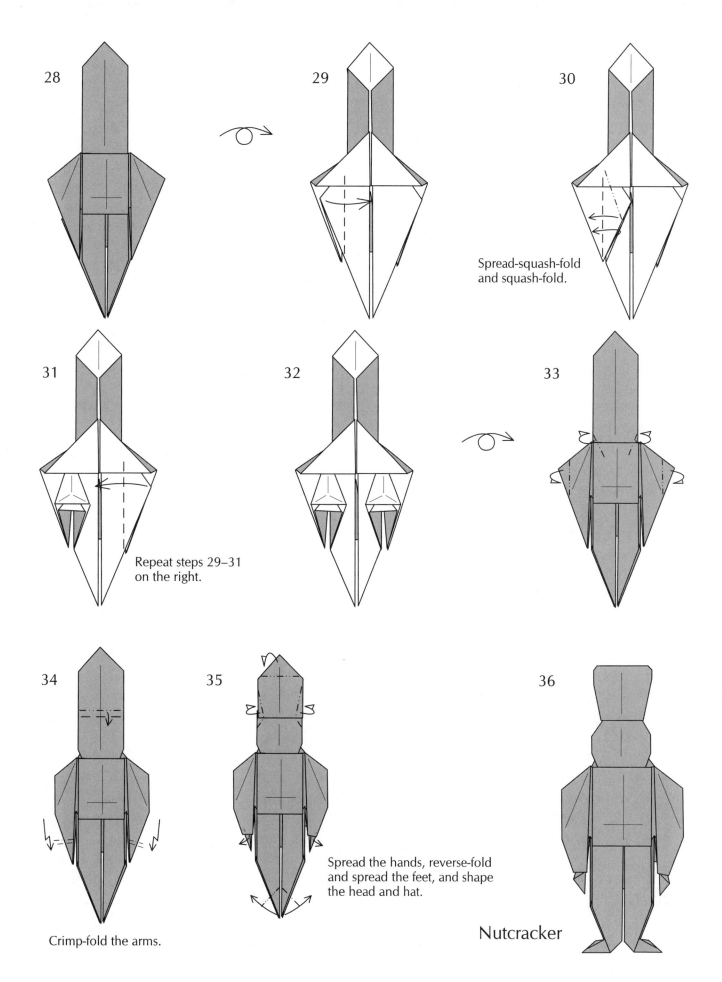

28

29

30

Spread-squash-fold
and squash-fold.

31

Repeat steps 29–31
on the right.

32

33

34

Crimp-fold the arms.

35

Spread the hands, reverse-fold
and spread the feet, and shape
the head and hat.

36

Nutcracker

Christmas Present

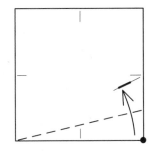

We wish you a Merry Christmas;
We wish you a Merry Christmas;
We wish you a Merry Christmas and a Happy New Year.
Good tidings we bring to you and your kin;
Good tidings for Christmas and a Happy New Year.

Oh, bring us a figgy pudding;
Oh, bring us a figgy pudding;
Oh, bring us a figgy pudding and a cup of good cheer: *Refrain*

We won't go until we get some;
We won't go until we get some;
We won't go until we get some, so bring some out here: *Refrain*

We wish you a Merry Christmas;
We wish you a Merry Christmas;
We wish you a Merry Christmas and a Happy New Year.

1

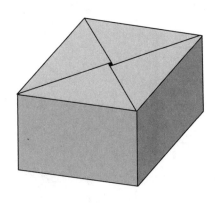

Make small marks by folding
and unfolding in half.

2

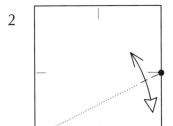

Fold and unfold on the right.

3

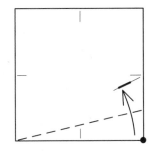

4

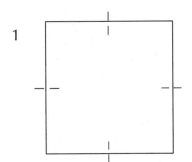

5

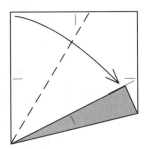

Unfold and rotate.

6

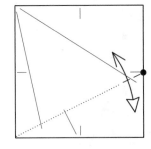

Repeat steps 2–5
three more times.

7

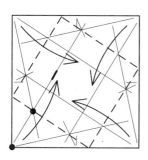

8

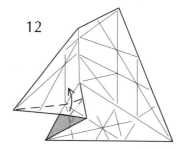

9

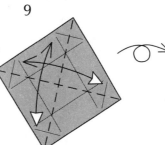

Fold and unfold.

10

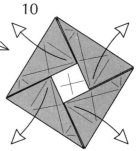

Unfold.

11

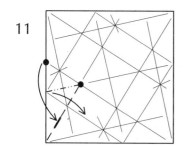

Push in at the dot
towards the center.

12

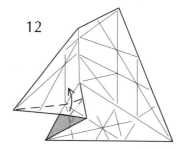

The model is three-dimensional.
Squash-fold.

13

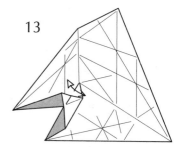

Fold and unfold. Rotate.

14

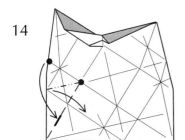

Repeat steps 11–13 on the
three other corners. Rotate
the corners to the top.

15

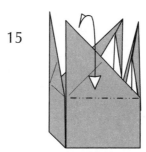

Fold and unfold.

16

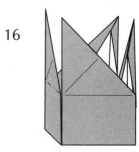

Repeat step 15 on
the three other sides.

17

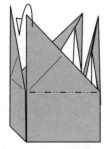

Fold down part of the way
to begin forming the top.

18

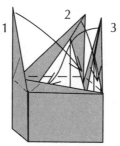

Continue folding the top parts down.
Each tab covers the previous one,
and the third one tucks inside.

19

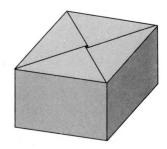

Christmas Present

Christmas Box

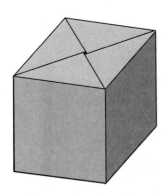

Deck the halls with boughs of holly
Fa-la-la-la-la, la-la-la-la
'Tis the season to be jolly
Fa-la-la-la-la, la-la-la-la
Don we now our gay apparel
Fa-la-la, la-la-la, la-la-la.
Troll the ancient Yule-tide carol
Fa-la-la-la-la, la-la-la-la.

See the blazing Yule before us.
Fa-la-la-la-la, la-la-la-la
Strike the harp and join the chorus.
Fa-la-la-la-la, la-la-la-la
Follow me in merry measure.
Fa-la-la-la-la, la-la-la-la
While I tell of Yule-tide treasure.
Fa-la-la-la-la, la-la-la-la.

Fast away the old year passes.
Fa-la-la-la-la, la-la-la-la
Hail the new year, lads and lasses
Fa-la-la-la-la, la-la-la-la
Sing we joyous, all together.
Fa-la-la-la-la, la-la-la-la
Heedless of the wind and weather.
Fa-la-la-la-la, la-la-la-la.

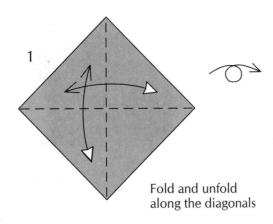

1

Fold and unfold
along the diagonals

2

3

Unfold.

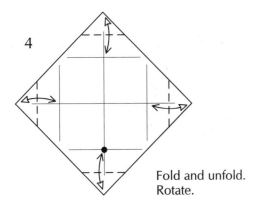

4

Fold and unfold.
Rotate.

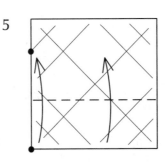

5

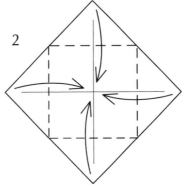

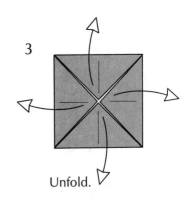

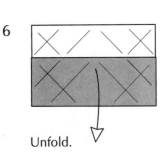

6

Unfold.

7

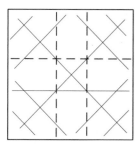

Repeat steps 5–6
three more times.

8

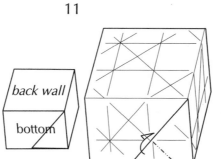

Fold and unfold.

9

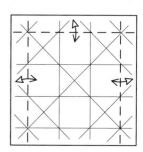

Fold and unfold.

10

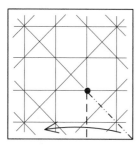

Push in at the dot.

11

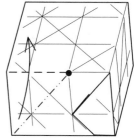

back wall

bottom

The small picture shows the
orientation of this three-dimensional
shape. Fold behind.

12

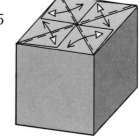

Repeat steps 10–11 three
more times. Rotate to view
the outside.

13

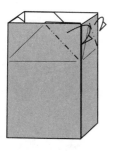

Fold behind four
times going around.

14

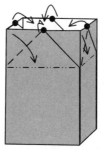

Collapse and flatten at the
top. The dots will meet.

15

Fold and unfold the four tabs.

16

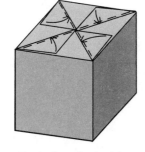

Tuck the tabs inside.

17

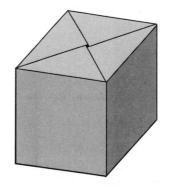

Christmas Box

Locomotive

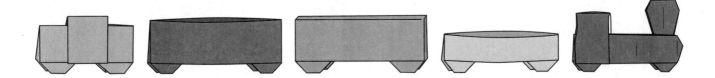

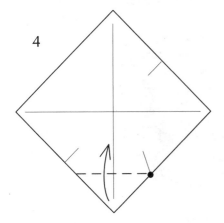

For this train set, fold each car from the same size paper. You can make a much longer train using one locomotive and caboose but several grain, freight, and coal cars.

Suggested colors are black for the locomotive and coal cars, yellow for the grain car, brown for the freight car, and red for the caboose.

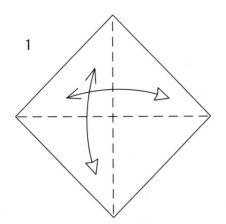

1 Fold and unfold along the diagonals.

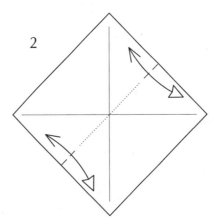

2 Fold and unfold at the edges.

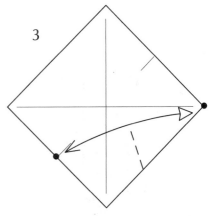

3 Fold and unfold creasing at the edge.

4

5 Rotate 180°.

6 Repeat steps 3–4.

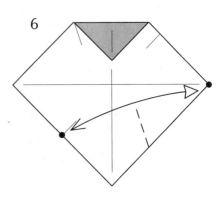

7

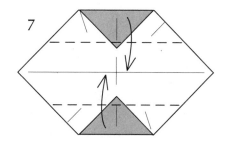

8

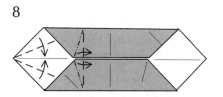

Squash folds.

9

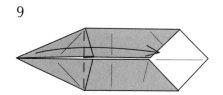

10

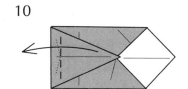

11

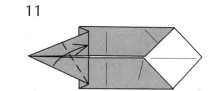

12

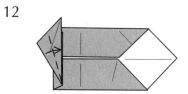

13

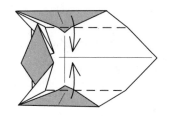

Unfold.

14

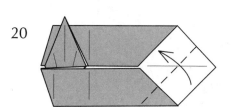

Repeat steps 11–13 in the other direction.

15

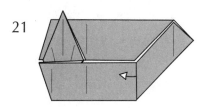

Unfold.

16

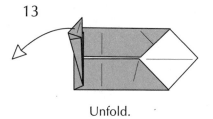

Unfold.

17

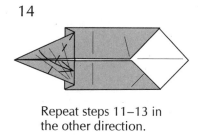

18

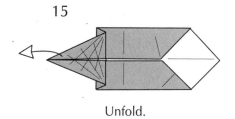

The model is three-dimensional.

19

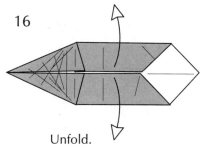

Flatten.

20

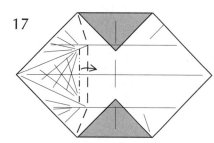

21

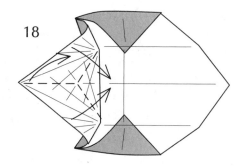

Pull out.

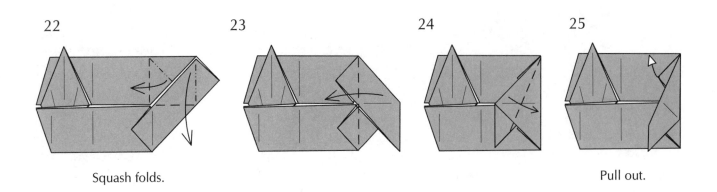

22 23 24 25

Squash folds.   Pull out.

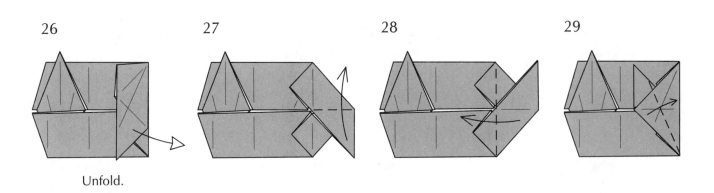

26 27 28 29

Unfold.

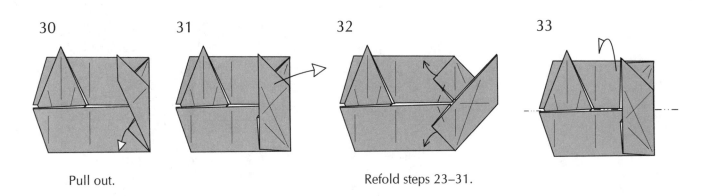

30 31 32 33

Pull out.   Refold steps 23–31.

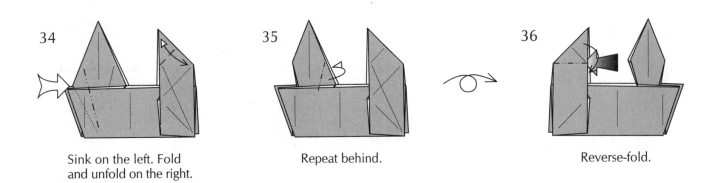

34 35 36

Sink on the left. Fold   Repeat behind.   Reverse-fold.
and unfold on the right.

37

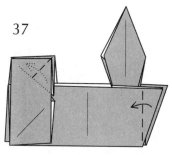

Fold both layers of the inside flap together. Repeat behind on the right.

38

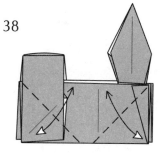

Fold and unfold creasing lightly.

39

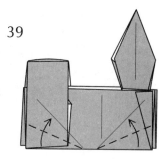

Repeat behind.

40

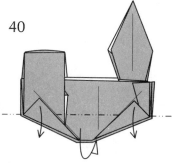

Repeat behind.

41

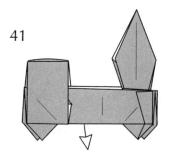

Unfold. Repeat behind.

42

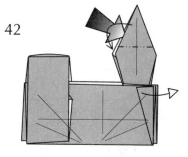

Reverse-fold at the top. Unfold on the right and repeat behind.

43

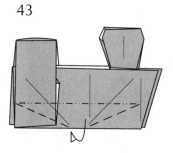

Refold and repeat behind.

44

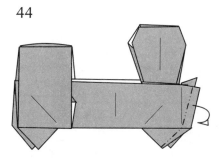

Fold behind and flatten. Repeat behind.

45

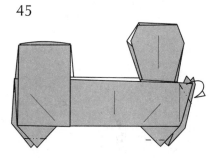

Fold inside at the bottom. Repeat behind.

46

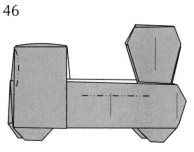

Crease lightly to make the locomotive round.

47

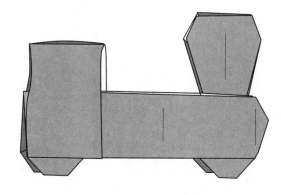

Locomotive

Grain Car

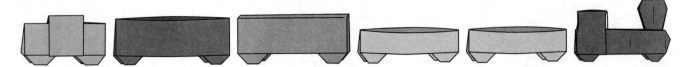

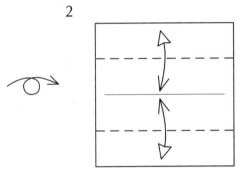

1

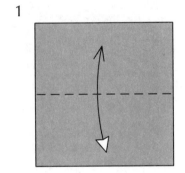

Fold and unfold.

2

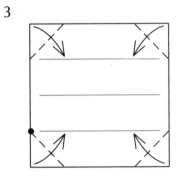

Fold and unfold.

3

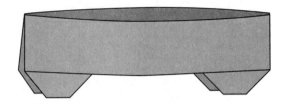

4

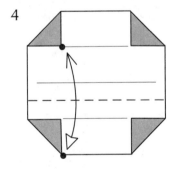

Fold and unfold.

5

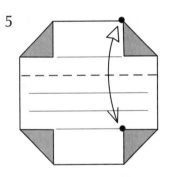

Fold and unfold.

6

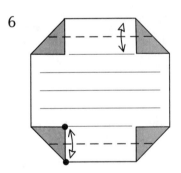

Fold and unfold.

7

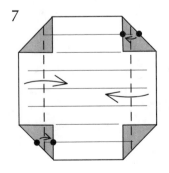

8

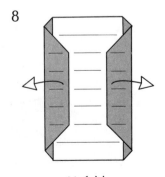

Unfold.

9

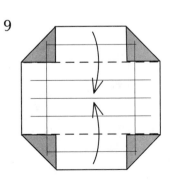

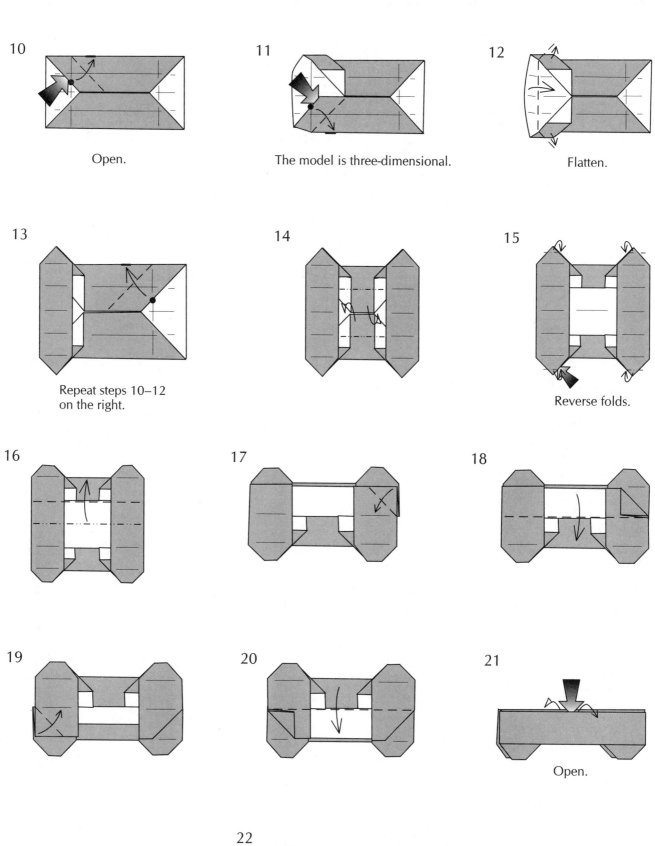

10

Open.

11

The model is three-dimensional.

12

Flatten.

13

Repeat steps 10–12 on the right.

14

15

Reverse folds.

16

17

18

19

20

21

Open.

22

Grain Car

Freight Car

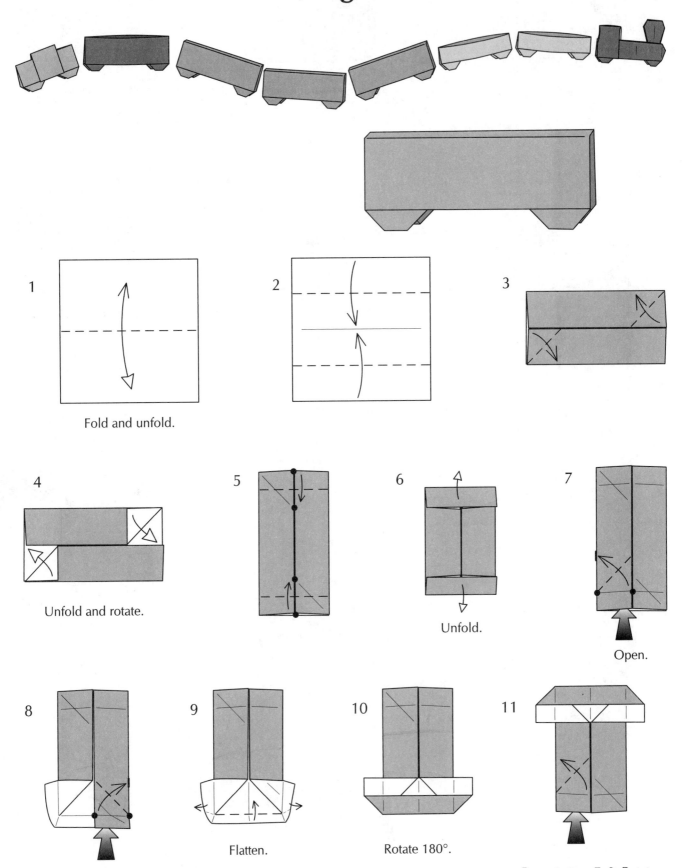

1 Fold and unfold.

2

3

4 Unfold and rotate.

5

6 Unfold.

7 Open.

8 The model is three-dimensional.

9 Flatten.

10 Rotate 180°.

11 Repeat steps 7–9. Rotate.

12

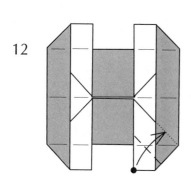

13

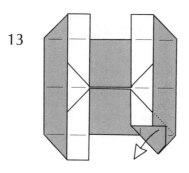

Unfold.

14

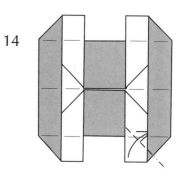

Reverse-fold.

15

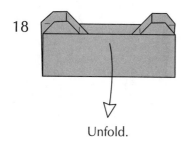

Reverse-fold.

16

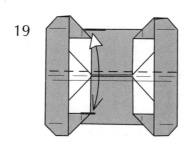

Repeat steps 12–15
three more times.

17

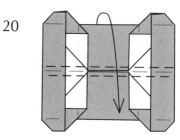

18

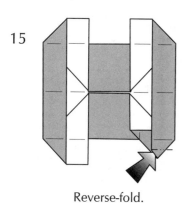

Unfold.

19

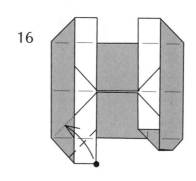

Fold and unfold.

20

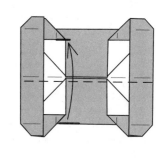

21

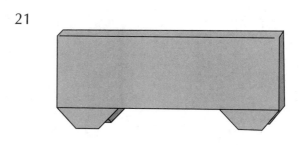

Freight Car

Coal Car

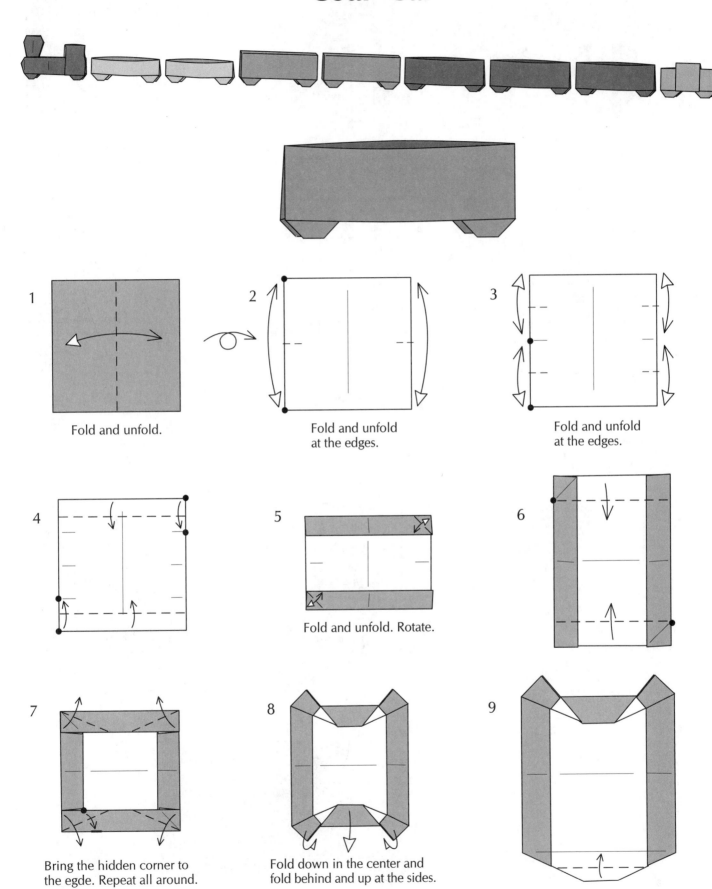

1 Fold and unfold.

2 Fold and unfold at the edges.

3 Fold and unfold at the edges.

4

5 Fold and unfold. Rotate.

6

7 Bring the hidden corner to the egde. Repeat all around.

8 Fold down in the center and fold behind and up at the sides.

9

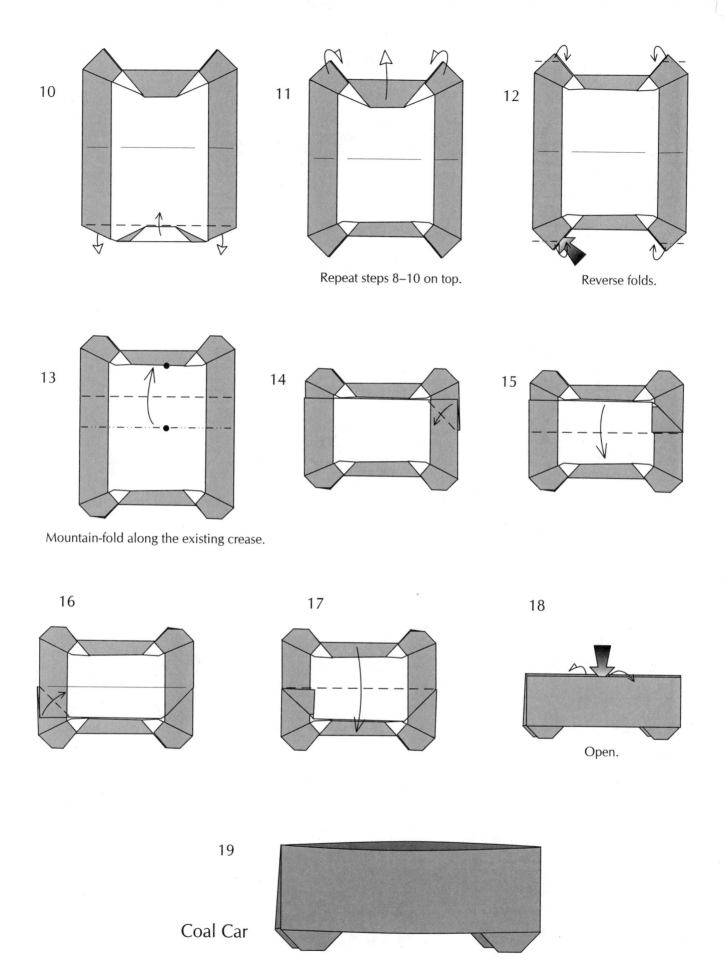

10

11

Repeat steps 8–10 on top.

12

Reverse folds.

13

Mountain-fold along the existing crease.

14

15

16

17

18

Open.

19

Coal Car

Caboose

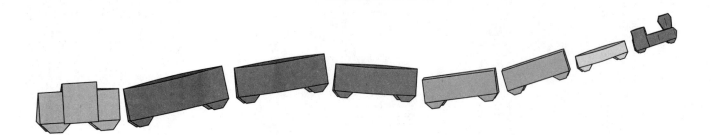

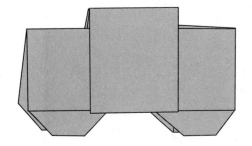

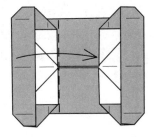

1

Begin with step 17 of the Freight Car.

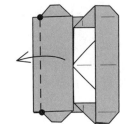

2

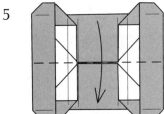

3

Repeat steps 1–2 on the right.

4

Unfold.

5

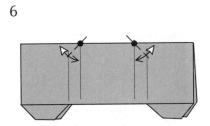

6

Fold and unfold all layers.

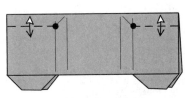

7

Fold and unfold.

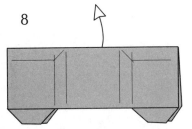

8

Unfold.

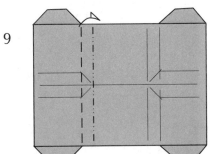

9

10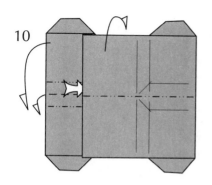

Fold in half and push in.

11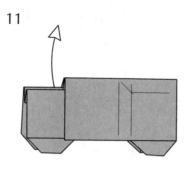

Unfold.

12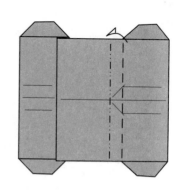

Repeat steps 9–10 on the right while refolding on the left.

13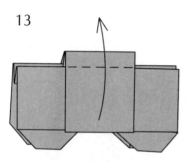

Crease lightly.

14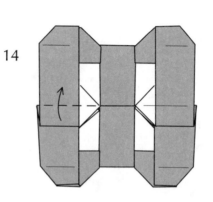

15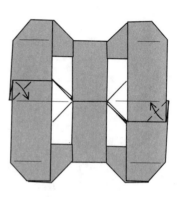

16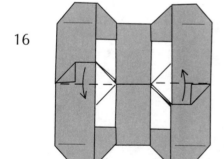

17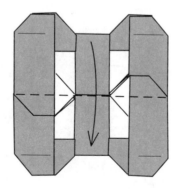

18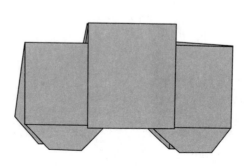

Caboose

North Pole

House

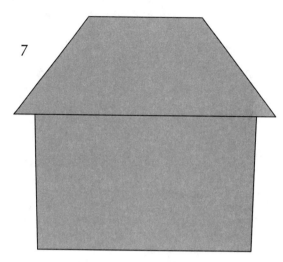

7

House

Over the river and through the woods
To Grandmother's house we go.
The horse knows the way to carry the sleigh
Through white and drifted snow.

Over the river and through the woods,
Oh, how the wind does blow.
It stings the toes and bites the nose
As over the ground we go.

Over the river and through the woods
To have a full day of play.
Oh, hear the bells ringing ting-a-ling-ling,
For it is Christmas Day.

Over the river and through the woods,
Trot fast my dapple gray;
Spring o'er the ground just like a hound,
For this is Christmas Day.

Over the river and through the woods
And straight through the barnyard gate.
It seems that we go so dreadfully slow;
It is so hard to wait.

Over the river and through the woods,
Now Grandma's cap I spy.
Hurrah for fun; the pudding's done;
Hurrah for the pumpkin pie.

1

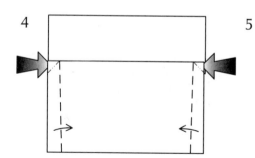

Fold near the bottom.
There are no landmarks.

2

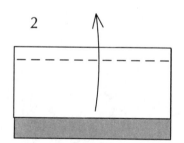

There are no landmarks.

3

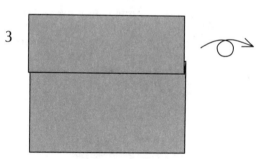

4

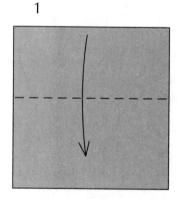

Make two squash
folds at a slight angle.

5

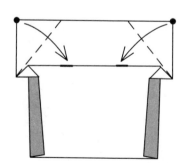

Bring the corners to the line.

6

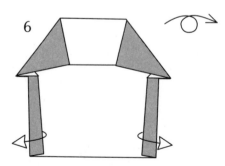

Open slightly for
the house to stand.

Mouse

A Visit from St. Nicholas
Clement Clarke Moore, 1823

'Twas the night before Christmas, when all through the house
Not a creature was stirring, not even a mouse;
The stockings were hung by the chimney with care,
In hopes that St. Nicholas soon would be there;

The children were nestled all snug in their beds,
While visions of sugar-plums danced in their heads;
And mamma in her 'kerchief, and I in my cap,
Had just settled down for a long winter's nap,

When out on the lawn there arose such a clatter,
I sprang from the bed to see what was the matter.
Away to the window I flew like a flash,
Tore open the shutters and threw up the sash.

The moon on the breast of the new-fallen snow
Gave the lustre of mid-day to objects below,
When, what to my wondering eyes should appear,
But a miniature sleigh, and eight tiny reindeer,

With a little old driver, so lively and quick,
I knew in a moment it must be St. Nick.
More rapid than eagles his coursers they came,
And he whistled, and shouted, and called them by name;

"Now, Dasher! now, Dancer! Now, Prancer and Vixen!
On, Comet! On Cupid! On, Donner and Blitzen!
To the top of the porch! to the top of the wall!
Now dash away! dash away! dash away all!"

As dry leaves that before the wild hurricane fly,
When they meet with an obstacle, mount to the sky,
So up to the house-top the coursers they flew,
With the sleigh full of toys, and St. Nicholas too.

And then, in a twinkling, I heard on the roof
The prancing and pawing of each little hoof.
As I drew in my hand, and was turning around,
Down the chimney St. Nicholas came with a bound.

He was dressed all in fur, from his head to his foot,
And his clothes were all tarnished with ashes and soot;
A bundle of toys he had flung on his back,
And he looked like a peddler just opening his pack.

His eyes—how they twinkled! his dimples how merry!
His cheeks were like roses, his nose like a cherry!
His droll little mouth was drawn up like a bow,
And the beard of his chin was as white as the snow;

The stump of a pipe he held tight in his teeth,
And the smoke it encircled his head like a wreath;
He had a broad face and a little round belly,
That shook, when he laughed like a bowlful of jelly.

He was chubby and plump, a right jolly old elf,
And I laughed when I saw him, in spite of myself;
A wink of his eye and a twist of his head,
Soon gave me to know I had nothing to dread;

He spoke not a word, but went straight to his work,
And filled all the stockings; then turned with a jerk,
And laying his finger aside of his nose,
And giving a nod, up the chimney he rose;

He sprang to his sleigh, to his team gave a whistle,
And away they all flew like the down of a thistle.
But I heard him exclaim, ere he drove out of sight,
"Happy Christmas to all, and to all a good-night!"

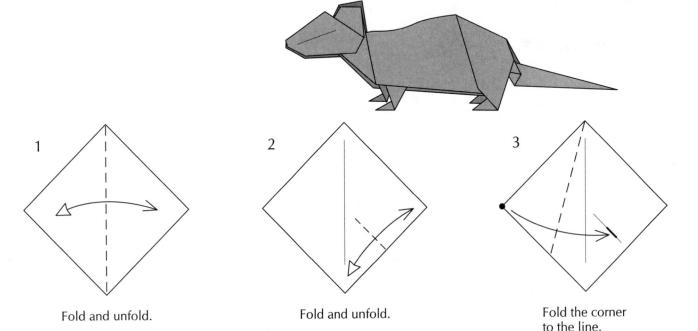

1

Fold and unfold.

2

Fold and unfold.

3

Fold the corner
to the line.

4

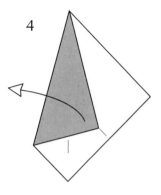

Unfold.

5

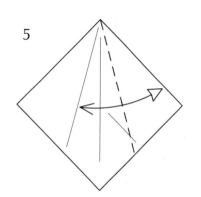

Fold and unfold.

6

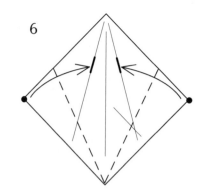

7

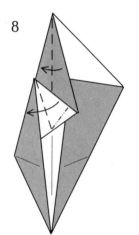

Reverse-fold.

8

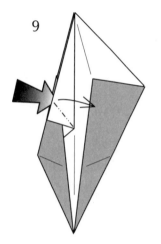

9

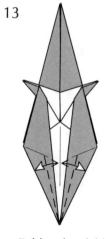

Squash-fold.

10

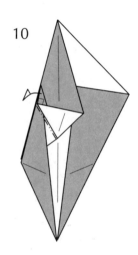

Note the right angle.

11

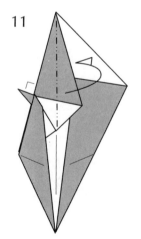

Note the right angle.

12

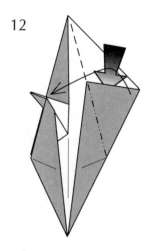

Repeat steps 7–11
on the right.

13

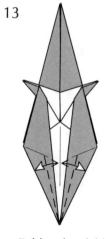

Fold and unfold
to the center.

14

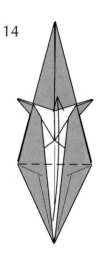

15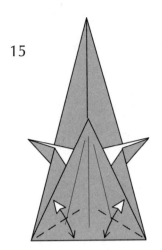

Fold and unfold.

16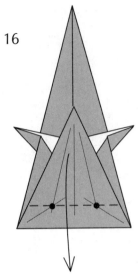

17

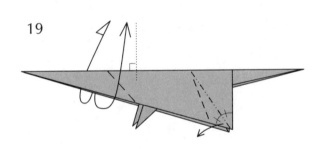

Squash folds.

18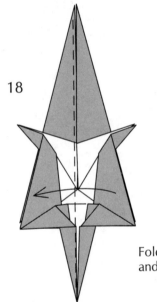

Fold in half
and rotate.

19

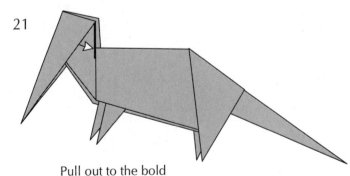

Outside-reverse-fold the head at a
90° angle. Crimp-fold the hind legs.

20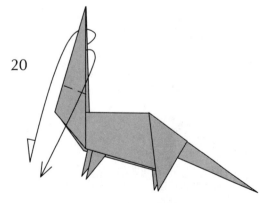

Outside-reverse-fold.

21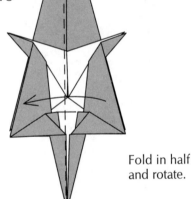

Pull out to the bold
line. Repeat behind.

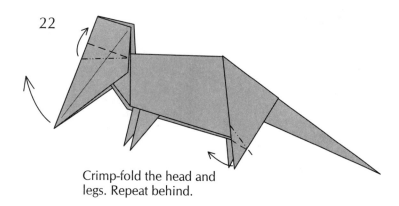

22

Crimp-fold the head and
legs. Repeat behind.

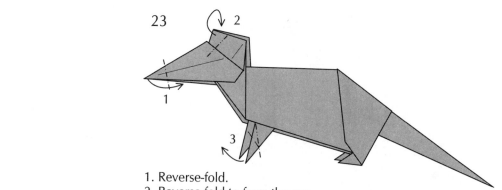

23

1. Reverse-fold.
2. Reverse-fold to form the ear.
3. Crimp-fold and repeat behind.

24

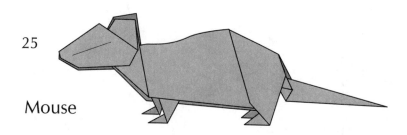

Fold inside at the head, and repeat behind. Make
reverse folds at the tail, and shape the back.

25

Mouse

Christmas Tree

O Christmas Tree, O Christmas Tree,
Your branches green delight us.
They're green when summer days are bright:
They're green when winter snow is white.
O Christmas Tree, O Christmas Tree,
Your branches green delight us.

O Christmas Tree, O Christmas Tree,
You give us so much pleasure!
How oft at Christmas tide the sight,
O green fir tree, gives us delight!
O Christmas Tree, O Christmas Tree,
You give us so much pleasure!

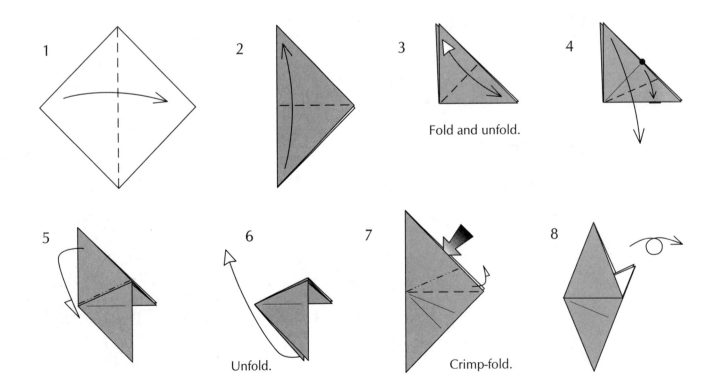

1

2

3
Fold and unfold.

4

5

6
Unfold.

7
Crimp-fold.

8

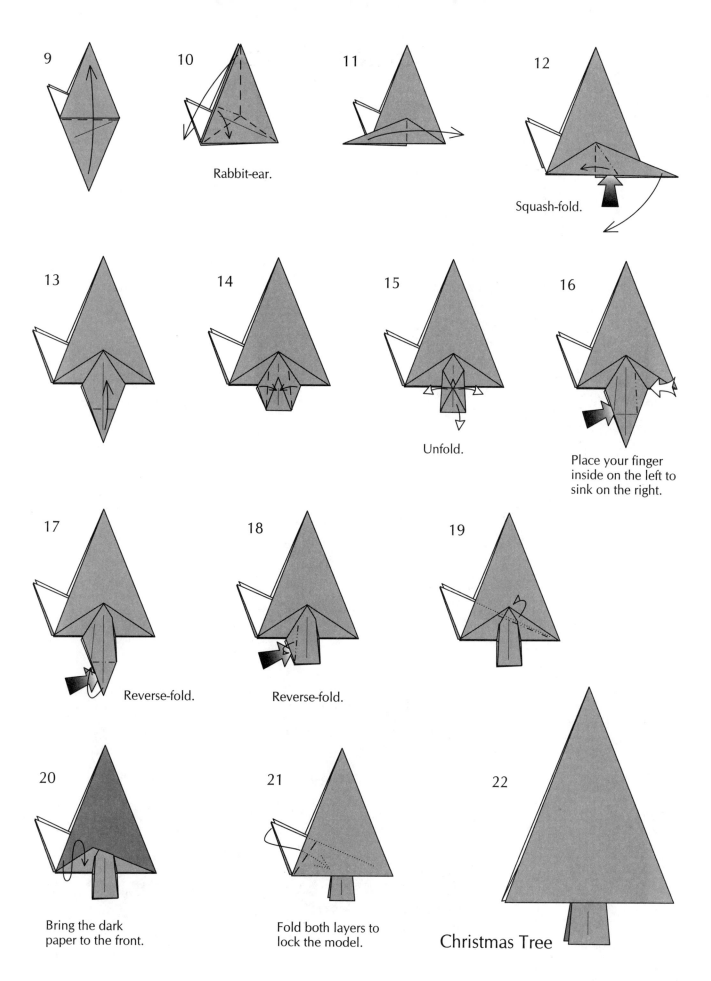

9

10

Rabbit-ear.

11

12

Squash-fold.

13

14

15

Unfold.

16

Place your finger
inside on the left to
sink on the right.

17

Reverse-fold.

18

Reverse-fold.

19

20

Bring the dark
paper to the front.

21

Fold both layers to
lock the model.

22

Christmas Tree

Winter Tree

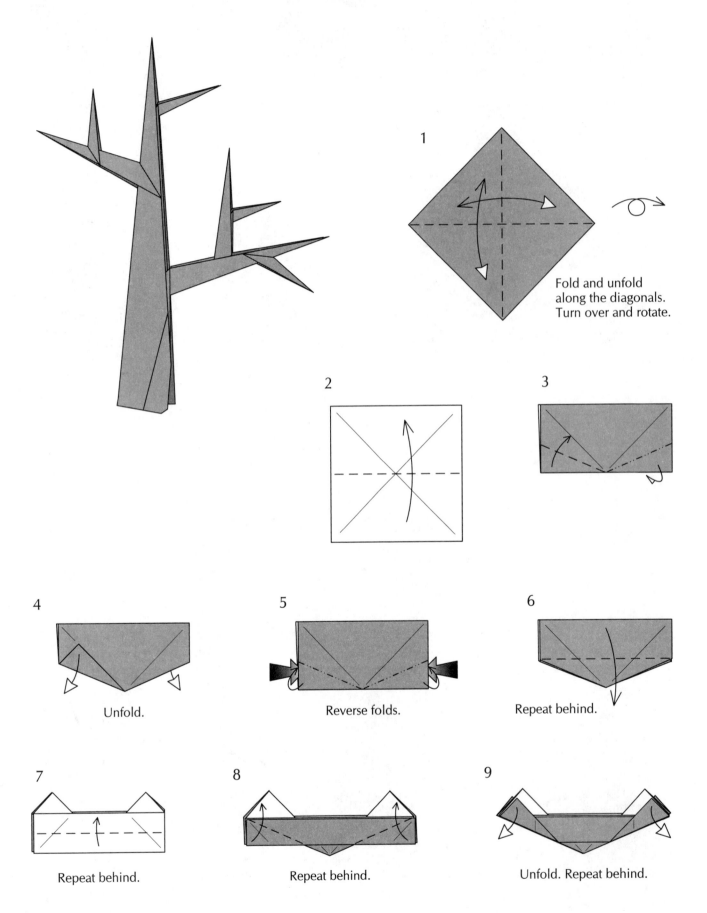

1

Fold and unfold
along the diagonals.
Turn over and rotate.

2

3

4

Unfold.

5

Reverse folds.

6

Repeat behind.

7

Repeat behind.

8

Repeat behind.

9

Unfold. Repeat behind.

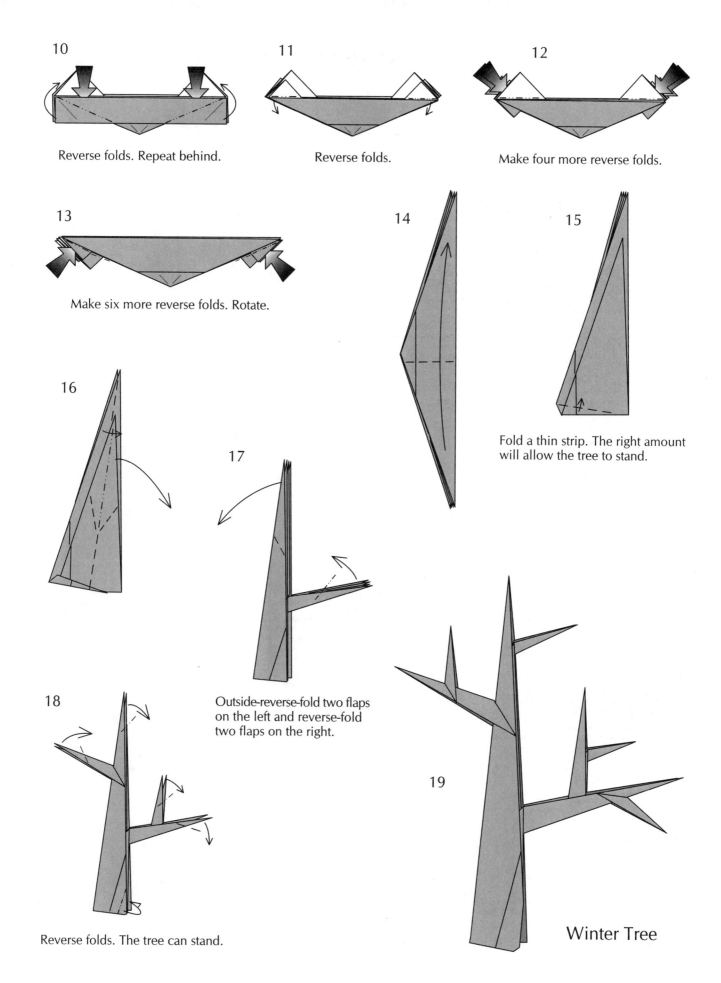

10

Reverse folds. Repeat behind.

11

Reverse folds.

12

Make four more reverse folds.

13

Make six more reverse folds. Rotate.

14

15

Fold a thin strip. The right amount will allow the tree to stand.

16

17

Outside-reverse-fold two flaps on the left and reverse-fold two flaps on the right.

18

Reverse folds. The tree can stand.

19

Winter Tree

Snowman

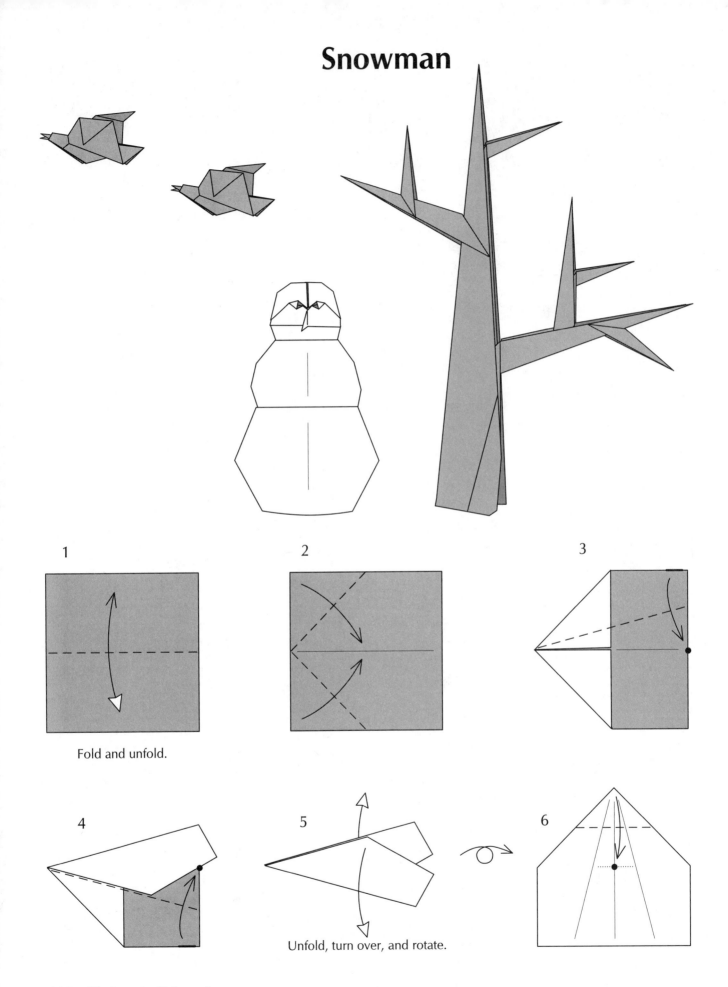

1

Fold and unfold.

2

3

4

5

Unfold, turn over, and rotate.

6

7

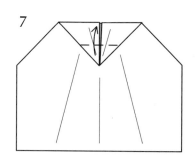

8

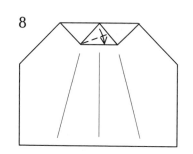

9

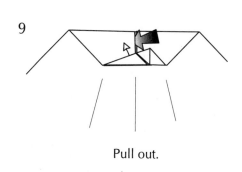

Pull out.

10

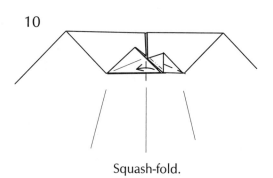

Squash-fold.

11

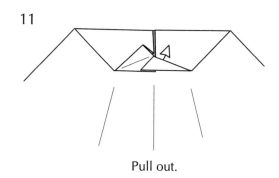

Pull out.

12

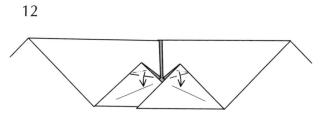

Form the eyes with squash folds.

13

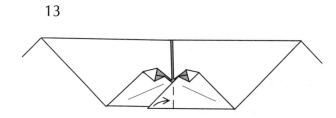

Fold the nose to point outward.

14

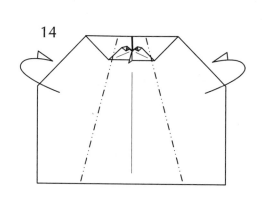

15

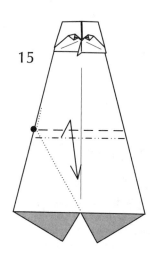

16

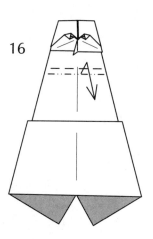

Snowman 111

17

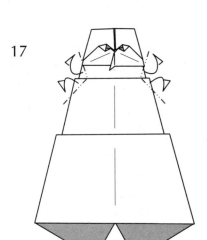

18

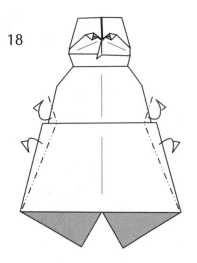

19

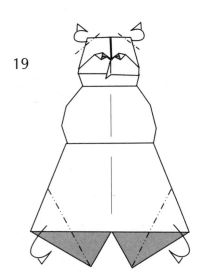

20

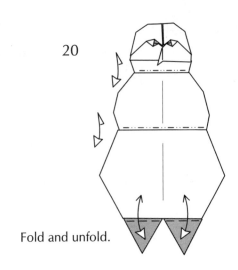

Fold and unfold.

21

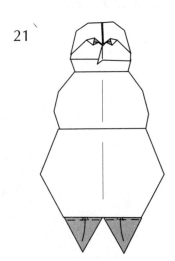

Tuck inside and spread a little at the bottom so the snowman can stand.

22

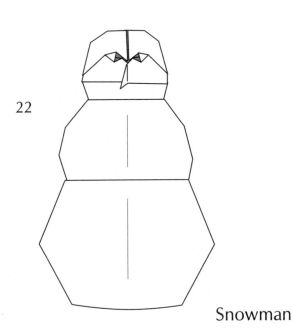

Snowman

Sleigh

Jingle Bells
James Pierpont, 1857

Dashing through the snow, in a one-horse open sleigh,
Over the fields we go, laughing all the way.
Bells on bob-tails ring, making spirits bright,
What fun it is to ride and sing a sleighing song tonight.

Chorus
Jingle bells, jingle bells, jingle all the way!
O what fun it is to ride in a one-horse open sleigh.
Jingle bells, jingle bells, jingle all the way!
O what fun it is to ride in a one-horse open sleigh.

A day or two ago, I thought I'd take a ride
And soon Miss Fanny Bright, was seated by my side;
The horse was lean and lank, misfortune seemed his lot;
He got into a drifted bank and we got upsot.
(Chorus)

A day or two ago, the story I must tell
I went out on the snow, and on my back I fell;
A gent was riding by, in a one-horse open sleigh
He laughed as there I sprawling lie but quickly drove away.
(Chorus)

Now the ground is white, go it while you're young
Take the girls tonight, and sing this sleighing song;
Just get a bob-tailed bay, two-forty as his speed
Hitch him to an open sleigh and crack! you'll take the lead.
(Chorus)

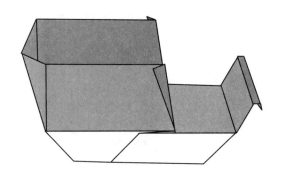

1

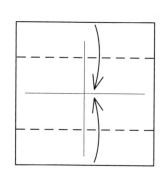

Fold and unfold.

2

3

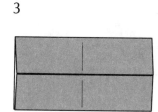

4

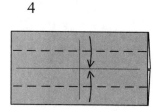

5

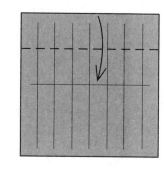

Unfold and rotate.

6

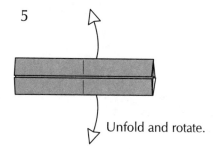

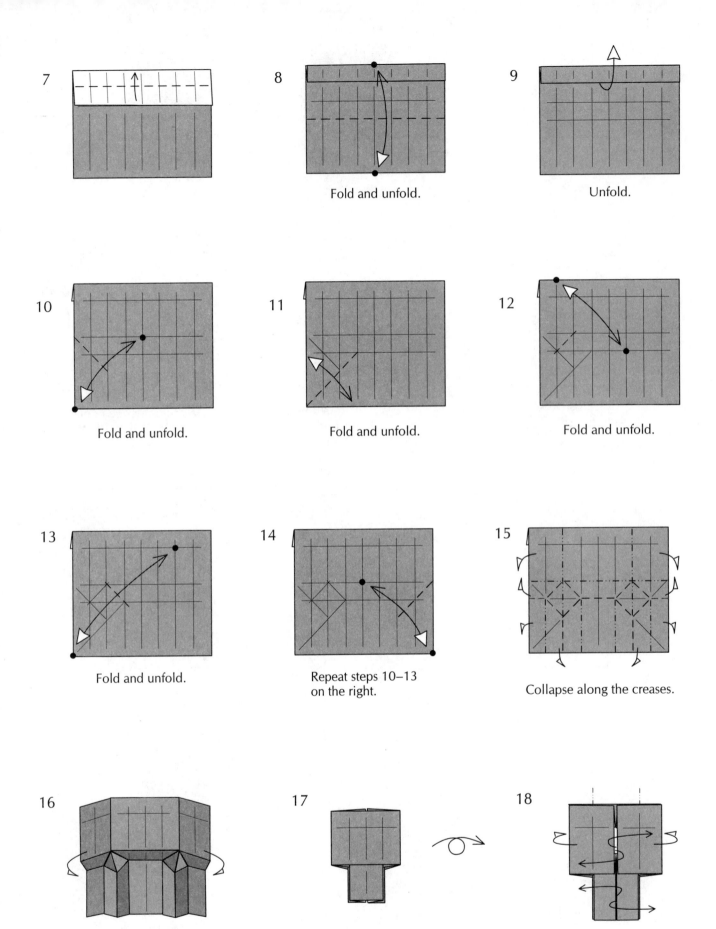

7

8

Fold and unfold.

9

Unfold.

10

Fold and unfold.

11

Fold and unfold.

12

Fold and unfold.

13

Fold and unfold.

14

Repeat steps 10–13 on the right.

15

Collapse along the creases.

16

Continue folding.

17

18

Open.

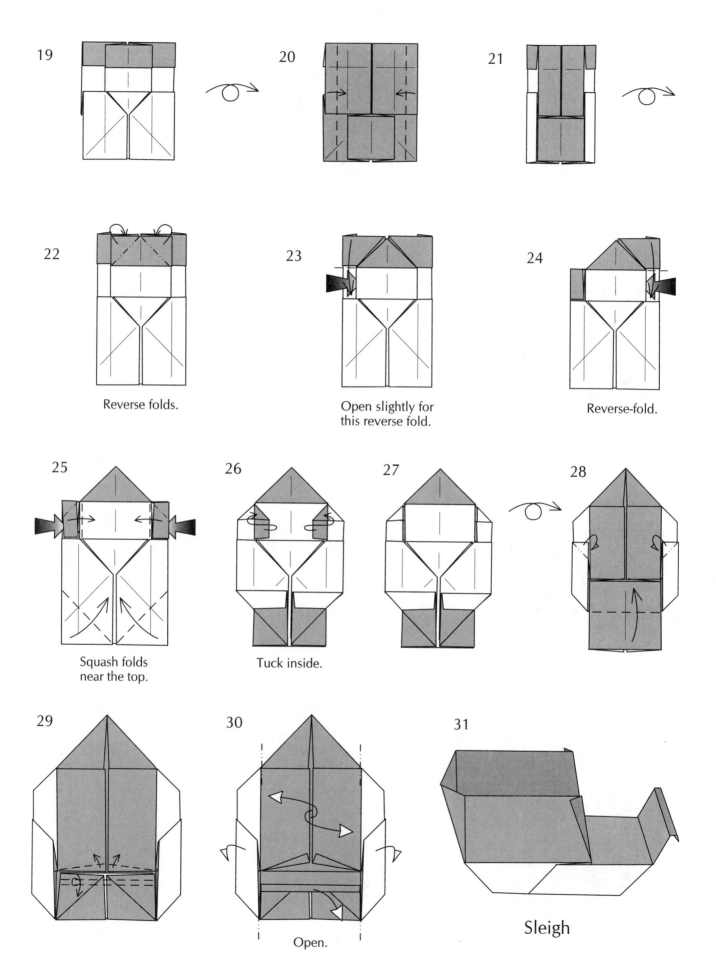

19

20

21

22

Reverse folds.

23

Open slightly for
this reverse fold.

24

Reverse-fold.

25

Squash folds
near the top.

26

Tuck inside.

27

28

29

30

Open.

31

Sleigh

Reindeer

"Now, Dasher! now, Dancer! Now, Prancer and Vixen!
On, Comet! On Cupid! On, Donner and Blitzen!
To the top of the porch! to the top of the wall!
Now dash away! dash away! dash away all!"

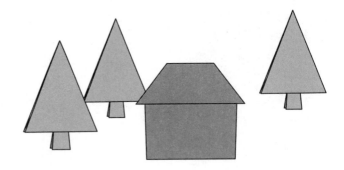

Begin with step 17 of the Cow.

1

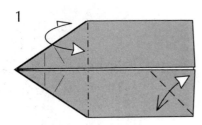

Fold and unfold on the left. Fold and
unfold the top layer on the lower right.

2

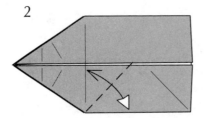

Fold and unfold the lower half.

3

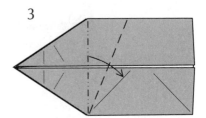

4

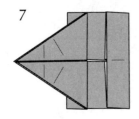

Unfold.

5

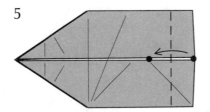

6

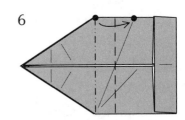

7

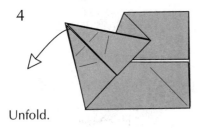

8

9

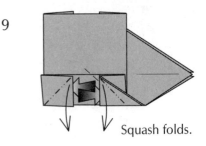

Squash folds.

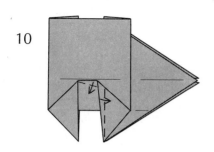

10

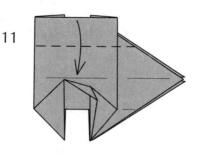

11

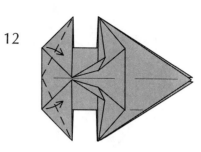

12

Squash-fold.

Repeat steps 8–10 on the top.

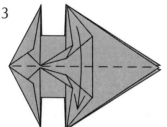

13

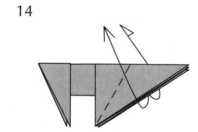

14

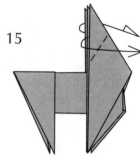

15

Outside-reverse-fold.

Outside-reverse-fold.

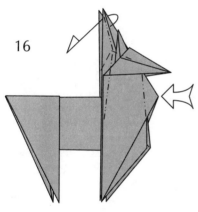

16

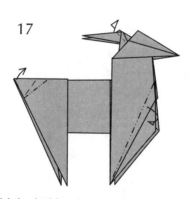

17

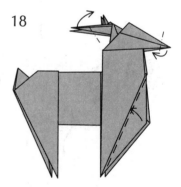

18

Sink the neck. Rabbit-ear all the layers together and repeat behind.

Fold the hidden layer at the horns, fold inside at the front legs, and crimp-fold the tail. Repeat behind.

Tuck inside at the legs, reverse-fold the horns and tip of the head. Repeat behind.

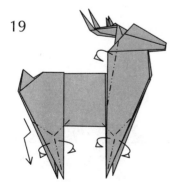

19

20

Repeat behind.

Reindeer

Santa Claus

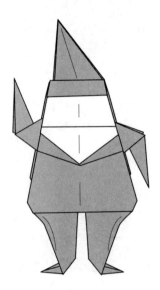

Up on the Housetop
Benjamin R. Hanby, c. 1860

Up on the housetop
reindeer pause,
Out jumps good old
Santa Claus.
Down thru' the chimney
with lots of toys,
All for the little ones,
Christmas joys.
Ho, ho, ho!
Who wouldn't go!
Ho, ho, ho!
Who wouldn't go!
Up on the housetop,
click, click, click,
Down thru' the chimney
with good Saint Nick.

First comes the stocking
of little Nell,
Oh, dear Santa
fill it well;
Give her a dolly
that laughs and cries
One that will open
and shut her eyes.
Ho, ho, ho!
Who wouldn't go!
Ho, ho, ho!
Who wouldn't go!
Up on the housetop,
click, click, click,
Down thru' the chimney
with good Saint Nick.

Next comes the stocking
of little Will,
Oh just see
what a glorious fill.
Here is a hammer
and lots of tacks,
Also a ball
and a whip that cracks.
Ho, ho, ho!
Who wouldn't go!
Ho, ho, ho!
Who wouldn't go!
Up on the housetop,
click, click, click,
Down thru' the chimney
with good Saint Nick.

1

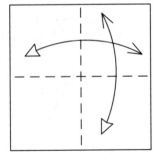

Fold and unfold.

2

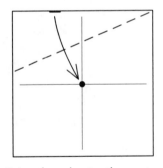

Bring the edge to the center.

3

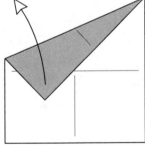

Unfold.

4

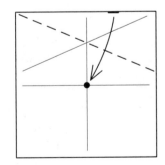

Repeat steps 2–3 on the right.

5

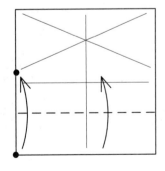

6

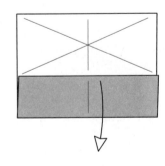

Unfold.

7

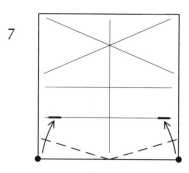

Bring the corners to the crease.

8

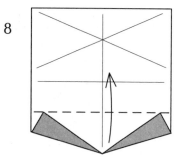

9

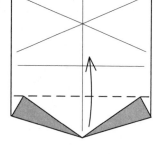

Fold along the hidden crease.

10

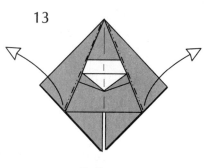

11

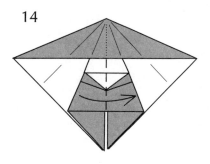

12

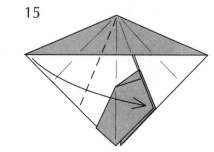

The dots will meet at the bottom.

13

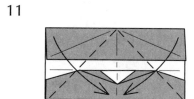

Pull out.

14

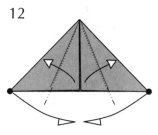

15

16

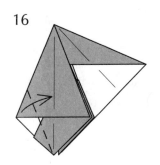

17

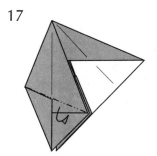

18

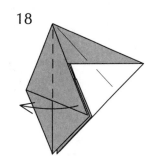

19

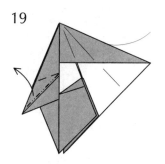

Squash-fold.

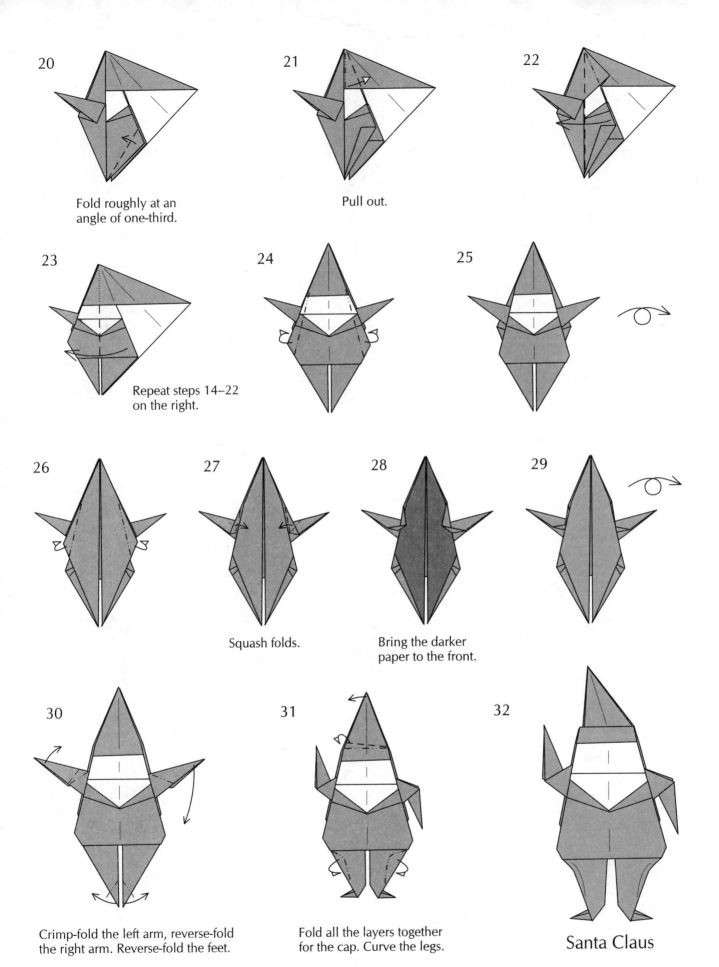

20 Fold roughly at an angle of one-third.

21 Pull out.

22

23 Repeat steps 14–22 on the right.

24

25

26

27 Squash folds.

28 Bring the darker paper to the front.

29

30 Crimp-fold the left arm, reverse-fold the right arm. Reverse-fold the feet.

31 Fold all the layers together for the cap. Curve the legs.

32 Santa Claus